THE GREAT EXHIBITIONS

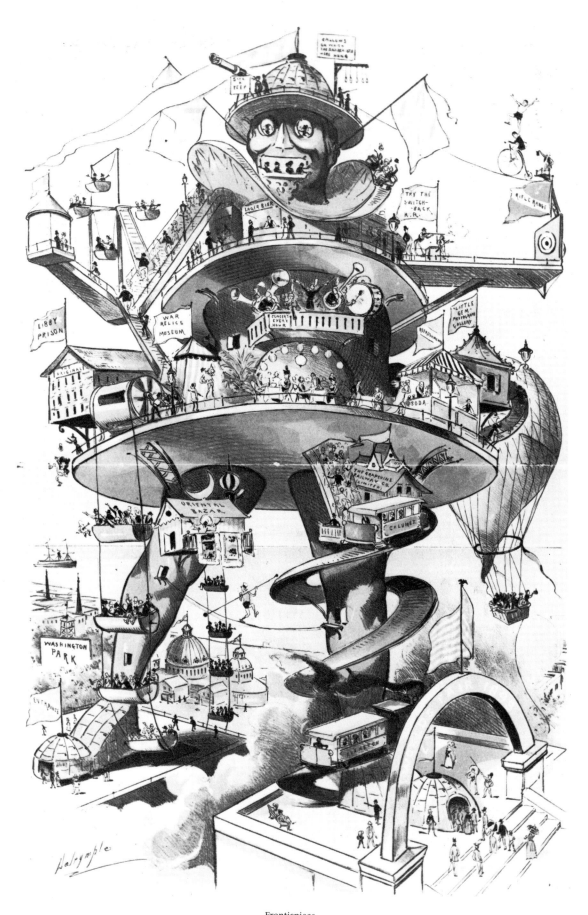

Frontispiece
'Puck's suggestion for the World's Fair – the *Colossus of Chicago* would knock out the Eiffel Tower.'
(*World's Fair Puck* 1893. Chicago Historical Society Collections)

THE GREAT EXHIBITIONS

— JOHN ALLWOOD —

STUDIO VISTA
LONDON

For Mary, Lucy and Jessica

All illustrations are from the author's own collection unless otherwise credited. The author would like to thank all those who have provided illustrations and who have helped him to trace the more unusual ones.

A Studio Vista book published by
Cassell & Collier Macmillan Publishers Ltd.,
35 Red Lion Square, London WC1R 4SG
and at Sydney, Auckland, Toronto, Johannesburg,
an affiliate of the Macmillan Publishing Co. Inc.,
New York

ISBN 0 289 70792 7

Designed by Anthony Cohen and Brooke Snell
Set in Monophoto Apollo 645 10 on 12 pt
Filmset by Keyspools Limited, Golborne, Lancs
Printed by Sackville Press Billericay Ltd.
Bound by Webb and Sons.

Contents

Preface

Apart from the large well-known headline-hitters, the last 125 years has seen countless international exhibitions, big and small. When one realizes that the Japanese delegation alone produced 96 volumes of description on the 1873 Vienna International Exhibition, and that the French Government even created a special department to write the official history of the 1889 Exposition Universelle, until a halt was called at the end of the twenty-first volume, it will be seen that to try to give a complete picture of all the international exhibitions from 1851 to the present day in one book is to put one's neck firmly and squarely on the block. Add to this the fantastic discrepancies that seem to lurk around every corner of historical documentation on exhibitions and it may be asked why anyone should even consider undertaking such a task. My hope is that this book will rekindle interest in these great activities which have been so sadly neglected. Few writers have dared to step into the international exhibition arena; most historians have been too busy chronicling 'important' past events to record the history of the efforts and experiences of ordinary men and women of each age. We cannot all be involved directly in the drawing-up and signing of great international treaties, but exhibitions give everyone the chance to participate in history, even if only as visitors.

I must acknowledge assistance from far more people than I can possibly mention without compiling another book, but the following, who gave particular help, have my grateful thanks, as indeed do all the others: Mr Robert Hatt, who did much of the detailed research in America and Australasia; Mr D.G.C.Allen, Librarian of the Royal Society of Arts in London, who allowed me full use of the Society's important collections on the subject; and Kay Walker who has typed the manuscript. Finally, and most important, my wife and family who have had exhibitions forced on them from morning till night and have had to contend with the birth pangs of every part of this book.

Introduction

Expositions are the time-keepers of progress.
The records of the world's advancement.
They stimulate the energy, enterprise and intellect
of the people, and quicken human genius.
They go into the home.
They broaden and brighten the lives of the people.

President William McKinley – introduction to the official picture book of the Lewis & Clark Exposition, Portland, Oregon, USA, 1905.

'A place where young people can see how rich the world is in ideas, how much there is yet to do, and the point at which we need to begin'. That is how Henry Ford described what may otherwise be known as an Expo, World Fair, *Exposition Universelle, Weltausstellung, Exposición Internacional,* or even International Exhibition. Whatever the term used, the meaning can encompass anything from a small local exhibition, trying to sound bigger and better than it really is, to a full scale Bureau International des Expositions Category One event, with up to eighty or more nations taking part and showing a complete cross-section of their achievements and life-styles.

Ford was, in fact, merely echoing the words used by Prince Albert to outline the basic intentions of the very first International Exhibition held in London in 1851 – 'The Great Exhibition of the Works of All Nations' held in Joseph Paxton's famed 'Crystal Palace'. Of the exhibitions that followed only a handful have ended the process with anything even approaching the profit that it made. Many have made diabolical losses and even more have left behind them desolate sites, unemployment problems and, in one case, an assassinated president. So why has mankind continued to hold such shows for the last 125 years? What unseen influence is it that drives humanity to spend its all in producing a bigger, better and even more splendid show than the last one?

When Henry Cole and Prince Albert set in motion plans for the 1851 exhibition, they were building on the combined foundations of the Industrial Revolution, the scope and reserves of the British Empire and the entire intellectual and social outlook of the period. Although they might not have realized it, they were also giving a new shape to a universal human attribute – they were making an exhibition of themselves or, more simply, showing-off. It is a trait much despised when found in the individual but the life-blood of commerce and industry.

Far from being a modern phenomenon this characteristic goes back to the roots of our culture. The Old Testament gives many instances of what was then the most acceptable form of showing-off – giving a feast. Of all hosts, the best known was King Ahasuerus, who ruled over the lands between India and Ethiopia, and who went to extremes in spreading his wealth and importance before his visiting nobles and princes. In the holiday feasts and markets of the ancient Greeks, held on the occasions of religious games like those at Olympia, and during political assemblies, the city states actually went so far as to allow hostilities to be suspended so that their enemies could trade and barter with them.

Even before then, travelling salesmen and little local village markets throughout the world had provided far more than the chance for the participants merely to buy and sell. Each market provided its visitors and traders alike with the chance to exchange news and participate in the highly human activity of 'one-upmanship'. In time some of these markets were to develop into the great medieval fairs, which were the focal point of regular annual holidays. They usually fell on religious festivals, which were almost the only excuse for any public holiday. The word fair is even generally agreed to be derived from the Latin word for holiday: *feriae*. In many cases these fairs were also the chance for local justice to be dealt out at the piepowder courts with their stocks and whipping-posts. Over the whole world, from Russia to England and from Africa to South America, the great medieval fairs with their wonderful mixture of trade, entertainment and theatrical experience grew in scope and size as communications improved and industry developed.

The International Exhibition movement, which followed on the fairs, was almost entirely concerned with industrial trade, and set out to 'forward the upward progress of industrial civilization'. The 1851 exhibition and those that followed it had the same aims; the exhibition of manufactured goods from various countries, in one place and in sorted categories, so that easy comparisons could be made. Until the introduction, in Paris in 1867, of some extension to this basic idea international exhibitions merely contented themselves with trying to be bigger or better than the previous ones. London in 1862 had far more, and in many cases far better exhibits than the 1851 exhibition but today who knows that there was an International Exhibition in London in 1862, let alone where it was or what the building looked like?

The first example of a true thematic exhibition was not seen until 1867. These displays with their linked themes gave the viewer more insight into a subject than a collection of miscellaneous objects with simple descriptive labels ever could, and were the beginnings of great changes in the presentation and objectives of international exhibitions. 1867 also provided the first instance of individual buildings put up at the expense of participating countries to house their exhibits in suitable national surroundings away from the circulation and display, to say nothing of competition, of the ever more massive main buildings. At the same time it gradually became less important to hold international exhibitions as a means of directly bolstering trade. They were increasingly used as gigantic vehicles for international public relations and the rivalry of whole life styles, rather than just in certain areas of manufactured goods or trade.

Eventually large private companies, and more recently the multi-national and international organizations, were to follow suit and make similar use of the exhibitions. This meant that it became less important that the whole event should make a profit for the organizing country. Indeed when the massive 1889 Paris Exposition Universelle made a profit the organizers and the public were surprised and taken aback – they simply had not expected it!

Following the switch from trade to public relations, international exhibitions have sometimes been held to try to revive or support failing, or failed, nations and empires. The French Exposition Universelle of 1878 and the more recent Festival of Britain in 1951 are good examples. In each case the exhibition helped to restore national pride and faith after a period of war and upheaval. Similarly the colonial exhibitions like those at Wembley in 1924–25 and Paris in 1931 set out to try and weld together fast-failing empires.

In any event, the motivating principle has been to show-off, to establish international status for the host country. Popular response has never been a prime objective, although even the biggest financial disasters have attracted crowds measured in millions. So today, public boredom with the genre can only be partly to blame for the question mark hanging over the future of international exhibitions. Only the exhibitions that have had new ideas to show or those that managed to find new audiences for the old ideas, like the Australian exhibitions of the 1880s and the Japanese exhibitions of recent years, have managed the sort of success almost automatically expected after 1851. Far greater threats to future expositions are posed by the lack of finance and cheap labour, an uncertain political climate, and the almost instantaneous communications of the modern world. Quite a few countries, such as America and Spain, have recently tried to organize international exhibitions but have failed through shortage of money. At present only Australia seems at all likely to carry out her plans, and that will not be until her bicentennial year of 1988.

But whatever their future, international exhibitions – from the overpowering designs and glorious eccentricities of the High Victorian period via the columns and valaria of the 1920s and 1930s to the publicity designs of today – have been glittering occasions. Each one, as Prince Albert said in 1851, has been 'a true text and a living picture of the point of development at which the whole of mankind has arrived', although sometimes the pictures they have reflected have not been quite those intended by the organizers!

8

CHAPTER ONE
The Beginnings

All Mud and mirth, and gingerbread, and joy;
Prancing in puddles, passing thro' each pen,
Into that Babylon of booths – the Fair.

St Bartholomew's Fair, 1816, Anon

It used to be shouted by the stall-holder:

Show 'em up, show 'em up, Ladies and Gemmens, for to see this extraordinary man that was never seen before and won't be seen again, and never will be seen at all if you do not see him now. (1)

Now it's written by a Public Relations Consultant in a glossy printed brochure:

Add your voice to this ringing, challenging shout of hope.
Let your eyes share in the vision.
And feel your heart beat just a little more rapidly.
For every age.
For every wish.
The celebration of tomorrow's fresh new environment.
Deep breaths become real again.
So does optimism.
And magic.
I am Expo '74. (2)

It all adds up to the same thing: if you don't pay your money you are going to miss the greatest event it will ever be your privilege to be invited to attend.

Of course, whether it really is the greatest is a matter of individual judgement. But be it a country fair of yesterday or a world's fair of tomorrow there are two basic ingredients which are essential for success – showmanship and people, an audience. It is only when the two are in the correct proportions that the goal of some of the organizers – a profit – is achieved. The first fairs were almost exclusively for the purposes of buying and selling. Originally the amusements were sideshows to the main business of trading, but at a time when a journey of twenty miles or more was a major adventure, the fairs also served as meeting places. It was the hangers-on and entertainers, taking advantage of the crowds, who stimulated the growth of the sideshows.

Today fairs have come to be pure entertainment, while modern industrial exhibitions, with commercial travellers and salesmen, have taken over the early marketing role of the fairs. All their emphasis is on trade which leaves little room for the jollity of the old fairs.

Whilst fairs were basically market places, exhibitions have always been primarily concerned with the display of goods. Fisher's *Accurate New Spelling Dictionary and Expositor of the English Language* published in 1773, gives the significant difference in a few words: a Fair is defined as 'an annual free market' whilst an Exhibition is only 'a displaying, a setting forth'.

European fairs were international in character virtually from the beginning, but England's insularity ensured her fairs remained almost entirely national. The Royal Society of Arts in London, formed in 1754 and one of Britain's learned societies, had a brief to encourage 'the arts, manufactures and commerce'. Accordingly it purchased the award-winning exhibits from its annual prize giving in 1761 and placed them on show for a fortnight in a warehouse. Thus England, the birthplace of the Industrial Revolution, held her first industrial exhibition. This proved such a success that although it had to be removed to the Society's rooms at the end of the two week period, it ran for a further five

1. Frost Fair on the Thames, London. (George Cruikshank – *The Comic Almanack*, 1838)

weeks. As a result, the Society decided to rent and equip a permanent exhibition hall. Thirteen years later the Society moved to its present premises designed by the Adam brothers, which included a special room for the 'repository'. Later it spent many years as the Society's Library, but it is now in use again for exhibitions and meetings.

Although England was first to show industrial inventions and processes at an exhibition, it was France which held the first real industrial exhibitions, displaying the products of industry rather than the methods of production. Following the Revolution and massive depression, the Marquis d'Avèze, Commissioner of the three former Royal Manufactories – the Sèvres porcelain works, the Gobelins tapestry works, and the Savonneries carpet factory – found himself with many unsold items on his hands and no purchasers. In a desperate attempt to find a market, he decided to arrange a special display of the goods at the great Château de St Cloud with a lottery featuring some of the exhibits as prizes. Unfortunately Bonaparte, fearing an uprising, ordered him to leave Paris the night before the official opening of the exhibition. However he finally managed to hold the exhibition in 1797 in the Hôtel d'Orsay in Paris and added many other trades to the original three.

The exhibition was such a success that the French Government, through its Minister François de Neufchâteau, the man responsible for the establishment of the Louvre Museum, announced an annual series of exhibitions. The first was held during 1798 in specially built exhibition buildings in the Champ de Mars on the banks of the River Seine. The three day exhibition was arranged to impress upon the visitor the ability of French industry to compete with the British. The catalogue and official report, which were a feature of this and subsequent French National Exhibitions, went so far as to say that French Manufactures were in fact superior to the English in many areas, although no comparisons

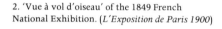

2. 'Vue à vol d'oiseau' of the 1849 French National Exhibition. (*L'Exposition de Paris 1900*)

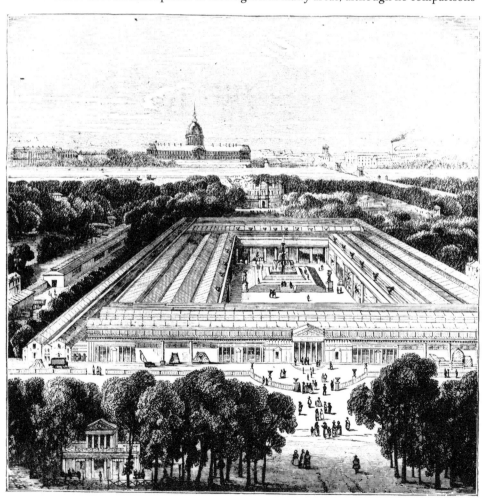

Opposite
3. The French National Exhibitions – (1) 1798, (2) 1801, (3) 1806, (4) 1834, (5) 1844. (*L'Exposition de Paris 1900*)

10

were made. 'Our manufactures are the arsenals which will supply us with the weapons most fatal to British power', said Neufchâteau. The occasion fell on the anniversary of the founding of the Republic and took place on the grounds of Bonaparte's triumphant victory parade on his return from Italy, and was a great success. It had been intended to hold annual National Exhibitions but the generally worsening international feeling towards France and the increasingly scandal-torn Directory led to no further mention of the projects until the formation of the Consulate in 1799. It was not until 1801 that the second exhibition in the series was held. The site this time was the courtyard of the Louvre and twice the number of exhibitors took part in a show which lasted six days. The exhibition ranged over the whole gamut of French production including ceramics and glass, textiles, furniture, chemicals, weapons and technical equipment and, for the first time, a live cattle section. M. Jacquard's loom, subsequently purchased outright by the French Government, made its first appearance among the many exhibits related to the textile trade.

The French National Exhibitions continued at irregular intervals, depending on the current political and international climate. Until 1827 they were held in the courtyard and subsequently the interior of the Louvre, except for the 1806 Exhibition which was held on the Esplanade des Invalides. In 1834 the venue was altered to the Place de La Concorde and the last three exhibitions of the series were held in the Champs Elysées. Both the duration and number of exhibitors gradually increased over the years until the eleventh and last exhibition in 1849 which had over 4,500 exhibitors and remained open for six months. Meanwhile in England several attempts were made to organize similar exhibitions. The first of these was 'The National Repository for the Exhibition of New and Improved Productions of the Artisans and Manufacturers of the United Kingdom', a semi-permanent show which opened in 1828 housed in a gallery running along the upper floor of the Royal Mews in Trafalgar Square where the National Gallery now stands. It was not well received by the public or the press who dubbed the 'new inventions and well-made British products' 'the toy-shop' and after some four progressively bad exhibitions the attempts ceased.

Other similar but smaller displays were held in the provinces and a successful Exhibition of Manufactures was held at the Free Trade Bazaar at Covent Garden Theatre, London, in 1845. But it was in Birmingham that Britain's first purpose-built exhibition hall was put up. This temporary building was erected for the annual meeting of the British Association for the Advancement of Science in 1849 and contained what was virtually the only exhibition of the French type to be held in Britain during this period. Indeed it nearly became the world's first international exhibition. Invitations to foreign exhibitors were issued, but no foreign exhibits materialized. However, it was visited by Prince Albert, and the following year the construction of Bingley Hall, which still remains today, commenced. Today Birmingham continues to lead Britain's exhibition facilities with her magnificent new National Exhibition Centre.

The lack of national exhibitions in Britain was not due to a deficiency of exhibits or ability, but rather to a complete lack of interest in what was seen, rather condescendingly by British manufacturers, as desperate attempts by the French to offset the effects of 'the undoubted superiority' of English products. M. Buffet (of station snack bar fame), the French Minister of Agriculture and Commerce, had suggested that the 1849 French National Exhibition should be international in scope but the French had lacked the confidence to carry it out. Thus it was the complacent British who finally found themselves holding the first International Exhibition and creating a genre of which one writer has said 'of all events in recent history, only wars have had more dramatic influence than World Expositions upon the expression of civilisation.' (3)

CHAPTER TWO
'This Cristial Exhibition'

So let us raise
Victoria's praise,
And Albert's proud condition,
That takes his ayse
As he surveys
This Cristial Exhibition

William Makepeace Thackeray 1851

After 1847 the Society of Arts organized annual exhibitions of 'select specimens of British Manufactures and Decorative Art' chosen from entries to its prize competitions. These became exceedingly popular with British manufacturers. The 1848 exhibition had 700 exhibits and 73,000 visitors and the 1849 exhibition was so large that although almost every possible part of the Society's small house was used, the categories of exhibits had to be limited. With encouragement from the Society's President, Prince Albert, all this activity led up to the organizing of a great National Quinquennial Exhibition in 1851 which was to be the first in a series of exhibitions based on the French pattern.

4. Part of the Turkish Section in the Crystal Palace 'displayed after the Eastern fashion'. London 1851. (*Dickinson's Comprehensive Pictures . . .* 1854)

5. Letterhead illustrating the Crystal Palace. London, 1851.

Henry Cole, an Assistant Keeper at the Public Records Office, had been involved with the Society of Arts prize competition since 1845. In 1849 he visited the French National Exhibition with Digby Wyatt who had been asked by the Society of Arts to prepare a report on this latest Paris Exhibition, and while there, they heard of M. Buffet's unsuccessful attempt to make it international in scope. On their return to England Cole had the opportunity to discuss with Prince Albert the possibility of making the London exhibition an international one. Prince Albert's decision was unequivocal. 'It must embrace foreign productions.' It would be 'international certainly.' (1) The interview ended with Prince Albert's request that Cole find the best possible exhibition site in Hyde Park.

A few days later, on 30 June 1849, an historic meeting took place at Buckingham Palace between Scott Russell, the Secretary of the Society of Arts, Henry Cole, Francis Fuller, a member of the original organizing committee for the National Exhibition and Thomas Cubitt, the founder of the building firm. (Fuller had also been to visit the 1849 Exhibition in Paris and had later met his friend Cubitt at Dover. At that time Cubitt was working on some alterations to Osborne House for Prince Albert, and so had the opportunity of talking to the Prince about the proposed exhibition and outlining his discussions with Fuller.)

For a pioneer and such a big undertaking, seven major decisions were taken very quickly at this first meeting. They were: that the exhibits would be in four divisions – raw materials, machinery, manufactured products, and sculpture and plastic art (no fine art would be admitted as the exhibition was to be industrial in bias); that a specially built temporary building should be used; that 'the vacant ground in Hyde Park on the south side parallel with and between the Kensington Drive and the ride commonly called Rotten Row, afforded advantages which few other places might be found to possess'; that the scope of the exhibition would be international; that substantial prizes should be offered to encourage exhibitors; that the organization 'would be by means of a Royal Commission, of which his Royal Highness would be at the head'; and finally that the organization of the finances, by means of voluntary subscriptions, should be undertaken by the Society of Arts. All these basic decisions were carried through, although medals were substituted for money prizes, and the Society of Arts relinquished its job of collecting the money to the Royal Commission.

After this meeting no time was lost in drawing up the necessary documents to present to the Government an official request for the setting up of a Royal Commission. Also during this period the feelings of manufacturers were sounded out and sixty-five towns in

England, Scotland and Ireland were visited, as well as contact being made with Germany and France. All this culminated in a great public meeting held at the Mansion House in London on 17 October 1849 when Henry Cole, as the Prince's accredited spokesman, outlined the entire scheme to the City of London's highly influential merchants and bankers.

Meanwhile the Society of Arts was trying to find the finance for the project. Fuller eventually managed to find two speculators, Messrs James and George Munday, who were willing to put up the money required to get the ball rolling for a return of 5% interest on the amount advanced plus a share of any profits. Finally on 3 January 1850 the Royal Commission was established and after five years of hard effort the Society of Arts was able to relinquish its responsibilities to a body which included four ex-Prime Ministers.

The Commissioners' difficulties were by no means over. Apart from lack of time, three major problems confronted them: the finding of the necessary money; the storm of protest, led by *The Times* newspaper and supported by members of both Houses of Parliament against the use of Hyde Park, and the presumed destruction of some of its trees:

> Albert! spare those trees,
> Mind where you fix your show;
> For mercy's sake, don't, please,
> Go spoiling Rotten Row. (2)

and the building itself.

6. 15½ foot high gas chandelier by Cornelius & Baker of Philadelphia. London 1851. (*Art Journal*, 1851)

A Building Committee was set up and it lost no time in inviting designs from 'competitors of all nations'. Although only three weeks were allowed for the designs to be submitted, 245 plans including thirty-eight from abroad, were received. The Committee chose sixty-eight of these for honourable mention but did not choose a winner. Instead, they prepared a design of their own based on the submissions. The gigantic edifice was to be built of brick and mortar and surmounted by a sheet metal dome suggested by Brunel, one of the Committee members. The design played right into the hands of the exhibition's detractors. The use of such building materials could only mean one thing: a permanent structure in their beautiful Hyde Park. They also claimed that there could not possibly be time to build such an enormous structure.

At this stage, Prince Albert, who was already depressed by the recent attack on Queen Victoria and the death of his friend Sir Robert Peel, almost gave up. However, a series of what can only be described as miracles saved the day. First a guarantee fund was set up which resolved the financial problem by supplying £250,000. Then both Houses of Parliament unexpectedly voted overwhelmingly in favour of the Hyde Park site. Finally, the solution to the building problem was provided by Joseph Paxton, gardener, confidant and friend of the Duke of Devonshire. The strong rib form of the 'Victoria Regia' water lily's leaf had given Paxton the idea for the supporting design of the greenhouse he built for it at Chatsworth, the Devonshires' country seat. This, and most of the other structural ideas he used in his design for the exhibition building, had already been tried and tested at Chatsworth, although there was a great difference in the scale and size. Throughout a railway committee meeting in Derby one evening, Paxton was observed to be busily scribbling on his blotting paper. By the end he had produced the basic design for his building in the form of a sketch elevation and section. He returned home to Chatsworth where he sat up all night producing an outline scheme to his own satisfaction, and the next day he wrote to the Society of Arts offering to give a lecture the following week on his design, which still barely existed! The ensuing eight days were spent in detailing the design with the assistance of William Henry Barlow, the resident engineer of the Midland Railway, and on 20 June Paxton took his drawings down to London.

On the train he met Robert Stephenson the famous engineer and a member of the Building Committee, and before long the large roll of drawings was undone and Paxton was going over his ideas. On the 22 June, the day the *Illustrated London News* published details of the official design, Lord Granville at the Board of Trade saw Paxton's plans and two days later Prince Albert saw them at Buckingham Palace. The Building Committee, however,

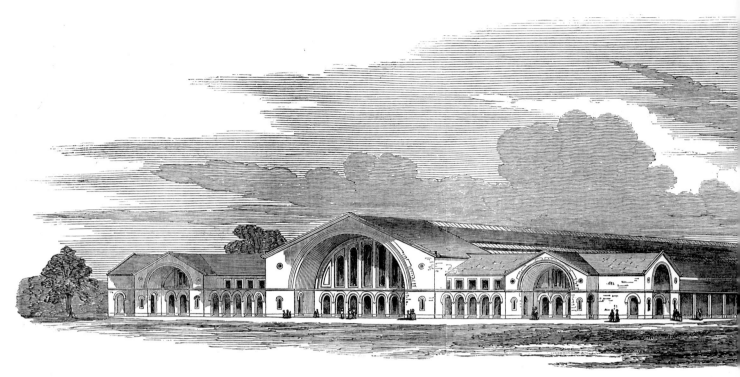

BUILDING FOR THE GREAT INDUSTRAL EXHIBITION, TO

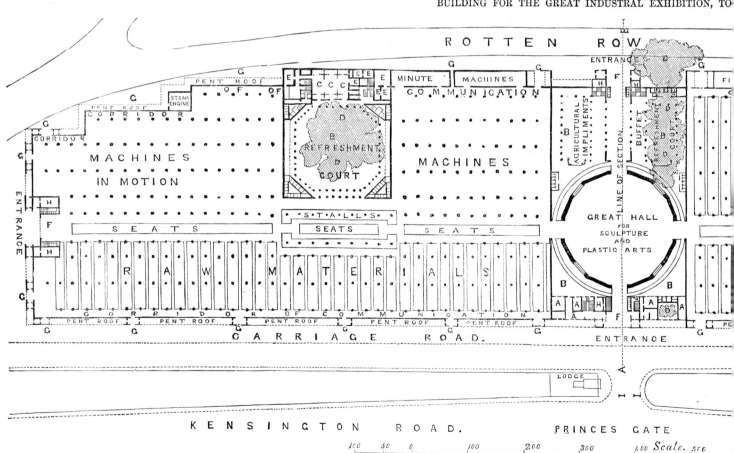

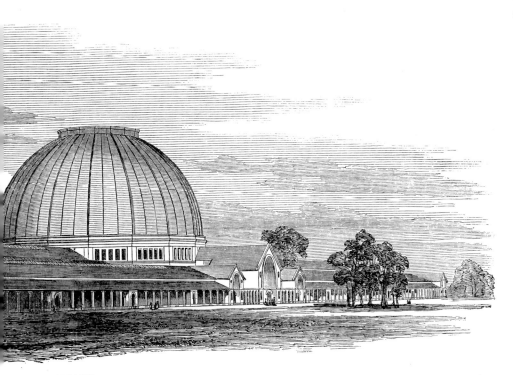

7. The 'original' design for the 1851 Exhibition. (*Illustrated London News*, 1850)

D IN HYDE-PARK.

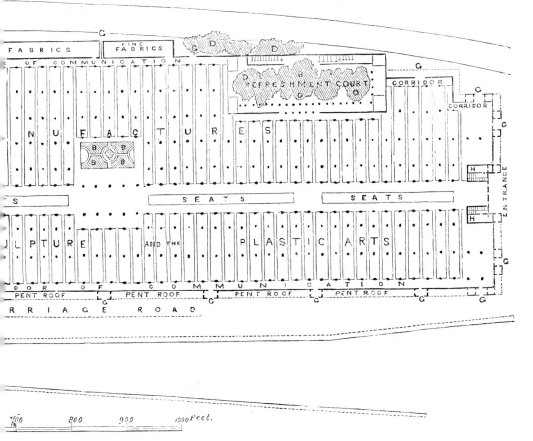

could not decide what to do. So Paxton decided to take matters into his own hands and arranged for his design to be published in the *Illustrated London News* on 6 July.

Public opinion immediately swung behind his graceful and obviously temporary building design. Official procedures, however, had to be observed and Paxton was eventually told that his design would be considered on the condition he had submitted a firm tender by the 10 July. Paxton had already contacted Charles Fox, a contractor; now Henderson, Fox's partner and R. L. Chance, a glassmaker, were urgently sent for. All three parties made a formal agreement and between them eventually worked out two tenders: one of £150,000 outright sale, and a second of £79,800 if the materials used remained the property of Fox and Henderson after the building was torn down.

As the official building was estimated to cost at least £100,000, and public opinion and the available timetable were solidly against it, there was only one possible outcome. On 15 July the Building Committee advised the Royal Commissioners to accept the Fox and Henderson £79,800 tender for Paxton's building and on 26 July the tender was formally approved. In the interim, the Commissioners had asked Fox and Henderson to increase the height of the building, still keeping within the original tender price, so that certain of the elm trees, so lately the subject of much public antagonism to the use of Hyde Park, could be roofed over. Paxton agreed and added a barrel transept to his design, based on his experiences with similar structures for the Great Conservatory at Chatsworth, and assisted by Brunel's exact measurements of the heights of the trees in Hyde Park.

No sooner was Paxton's design officially accepted than another tirade of antagonism swept across London. Prince Albert summed this up in his letter to the King of Prussia, who had written to enquire if it would be safe to visit London during the exhibition:

Mathematicians have calculated that the Crystal Palace will blow down in the first strong gale; Engineers that the galleries would crash in and destroy the visitors; Political Economists have prophesied a scarcity of food in London owing to the vast concourse of people; Doctors that owing to so many races coming into contact with each other the Black Death of the Middle Ages would make its appearance as it did after the Crusades; Moralists that England would be infected by all the scourges of the civilised and uncivilised world; Theologians that this second Tower of Babel would draw upon it the vengeance of an offended God. (3)

Prince Albert finished his letter by informing the King that he personally would be unable to guarantee him against these perils!

8. A Park phaeton by Messrs Hallmarke, Aldebert & Hallmarke of London. London 1851. (*Art Journal*, 1851)

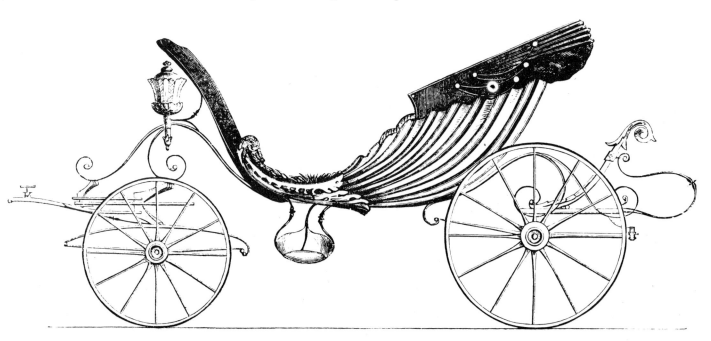

The contractors fixed the first column on 26 September 1850 and seventeen weeks later the building was handed over to the Commissioners. It says much for the spirit in which Fox and Henderson undertook the job that until the end of October they had no official instruction to proceed, because until then no one knew who was the correct person to issue such an order.

The great modular building was built of iron, glass and wood and it is worth noting, as did Charles Downes in *The Building Erected in Hyde Park for the Great Exhibition of the works of Industry of All Nations 1851*, published in 1852, that 'there are no *large* pieces of either material employed. The heaviest pieces of cast iron are the girders, which are 24 feet in length, and none of which weigh more than a ton; the wrought iron consists chiefly of round and flat bars, angle irons, bolts, screws and rivets. A large quantity of sheet iron is also employed in the construction of the louvres.

'Wood is used in the main gutters and Paxton gutters, the arched ribs of the Transept, the sash-bars and ridges, the ground-floor and gallery floors, the lead flats and the external wall, and in some of the girders or trusses. The glass is sheet or cylinder glass, in panes 10×49in., weighs 16oz. per square foot.' The 3,300 hollow iron columns, which also acted as drainpipes for the flat roof, and the 200 miles of sash-bars, as well as the 34 miles of patent Paxton guttering, designed to solve the problems of condensation, were all produced using specially designed and built machine tools, the sash-bars even being painted by machine. Meanwhile Chance Brothers in Birmingham were producing the 300,000 panes of glass, to a size larger than had so far been manufactured, ready for fitting by the glaziers riding high up in the open structure in their glazing wagons.

The whole building was a living example of the possibilities of modern mass-production techniques but to the people watching it rise in Hyde Park behind the wooden fence (formed from the timber later to become the floors) it had become the 'Crystal Palace': a name given to it by *Punch* magazine and echoed by the great plethora of poetry (and worse) which was already bestowing on it an almost mythical beauty, although the poems themselves were not always on such a level:

> But yesterday a naked sod
> The dandies sneered from Rotten Row,
> And cantered o'er it to and fro:
> > And see 'tis done!
> As though 'twere by a wizard's rod
> A blazing arch of lucid glass
> Leaps like a fountain from the grass
> > To meet the sun! (4)

Perhaps two of the least praised features of the Palace were the colour scheme chosen by Owen ('Alhambra') Jones who used primary hues to decorate the interior structural members, and the placing of the flags of all nations along the outside perimeter roof of the building, the idea of Charles Barry, an architect and member of the Building Committee.

Meanwhile Cole, Digby Wyatt and Wentworth Dilke, with the help of Dr Lyon Playfair, were busy selecting and collecting the exhibits. If the whole building had been given over to British exhibits, it would have been too small to take everything that was offered, and as half the building was to house British and the other half foreign exhibits, a system of selection was needed. In the foreign section this was left to the governments concerned once the exact area available to them had been decided, but in Britain a series of committees in each locality selected exhibits which were then finally passed or rejected by a central committee in London.

The actual classification system, which was based on Prince Albert's original three categories – the raw materials of industry, the manufactures made from them and the art used to adorn them – created many problems until Playfair resolved the situation with his thirty clearly defined and workable divisions of exhibits each with their committee of specialists to oversee the actual exhibit selection.

The problems of judging were much more involved because it was the first time international juries had attempted such a feat. The process was based on the French experience and the previous Society of Arts exhibitions and was carefully laid down but many of the juries' decisions seemed odd to say the least. Notwithstanding the short time available and the immense amount of work, often covering unknown territory, the administration of the exhibition by Henry Cole and his colleagues was magnificent and by the opening day all the British exhibits were in place and about nine-tenths of the foreign sections had been received. At half-past eleven on 1 May 1851 a procession of nine State carriages left Buckingham Palace:

A little rain fell, just as we started, but before we neared the Crystal Palace, the sun shone and gleamed upon the gigantic edifice, upon which the flags of every nation were flying. We drove up Rotten Row and got out of our carriages at the entrance on that side. The glimpse, through the iron gates of the transept, the waving palms and flowers, the myriads of people filling the galleries and seats around, together with the flourish of trumpets as we entered the building, gave a sensation I shall never forget, and I felt much moved . . . the sight as we came into the middle where the steps and a chair . . . were placed, with the beautiful crystal fountain just in front of it, was magical – so vast, so glorious, so touching. One felt . . . filled with devotion . . . The tremendous cheers, the joy expressed in every face, the immensity of the building, the mixture of palms, flowers, trees, statues, fountains, the organ (with 200 instruments and 600 voices, which sounded like nothing), and my beloved husband, the author of this 'peace festival', which united the industry of all nations of the earth – all this was moving indeed, and it was and is a day to live for ever. (5)

9. 'Odds and Ends, in, out, and about, The Great Exhibition of 1851'. George Cruikshank 1851.

A Gentleman who has unfortunately lost his party –

An Extra-ordinary great Visitor to the Great Exhibition –

A Party who have unfortunately lost their friend, who carried the basket of provisions!

Odds & Ends, in, out, & about. The Great Exhibition of 1851.

Thus Queen Victoria described the opening of the world's first international exhibition in her personal diary. It was the first time so many nations of the world had come together for such a peaceful purpose.

Queen Victoria's enthusiasm, and the overwhelming effect of the building and its contents on nearly all who visited London in that summer of 1851, have been repeated in many a written, sung or spoken word since. Through it all one senses the tremendous thirst for knowledge, faith in life and almost religious fervour which was displayed by the exhibition and the visitors themselves:

> Sheltered by crystal walls and roof, we view
> All products of the earth, the air, and seas,
> Assuming every texture, form, and hue,
> That can a man's corporeal senses please,
> And gladden Beauty's sense to ecstacies.
> Art unto man is a magician's rod,
> Prolonging life, absolving from disease;
> Extracting good from out the meanest sod;
> Rivalling Nature's works, and making him a God. (6)

Before we look in detail at some of the exhibits, it is important to understand the Victorian attitude to design. In the nineteenth century, designers as such hardly existed, their work being done by artist craftsmen and decorators. Almost without exception design meant decoration rather than function – the decoration of every possible facet and detail without much thought to the practicality of such finishes. It was almost always based on historic decorative styles, very often being a mixture of many of these. In basic form everything reflected the security of middle and upper class Victorian life (they were after all the potential consumers) in its solid and curvaceous forms. The Crystal Palace was a break away from current thinking if only because it was so functional. In fact, to the Victorians it was not an architectural form at all – it was pure engineering, to be compared with such masterpieces as Thomas Telford's Menai Bridge and Marc Isambard Brunel's Thames Tunnel.

It should also be remembered that each international exhibition is an occasion to produce not only the best and the most perfectly finished items but also the often over-elaborate special idea that has been merely a dream. The results of such opportunity can be seen as clearly in the exhibits of 1851 as in the extravaganzas of modern exhibitions. Indeed many Victorian items were so unusual in form and shape and so elaborately decorated that today it is difficult to guess their intended use – items such as the polished iron stove designed by Edward Baum in the form of a knight in full armour and displayed in the Prussian section of the Crystal Palace; and Dunin's Expanding Man 'intended to illustrate the different proportions of the human figure; it admits of being expanded from the size of the Apollo Belvedere to that of a colossal statue' (7); to say nothing of the collection of stuffed animals from Wurtembourg which Queen Victoria thought 'really marvellous'. Unusual materials like *papier mâché* and gutta percha were used in a wide variety of furniture and decoration, some practical, but many others not so. The exhibits were not exact copies of items in general use. They were produced to surprise, delight and amaze the visitor, in the same way that water-beds at furniture shows and nude females draped alluringly over cars at motor shows do today.

The nude statues at the exhibition probably provided the largest expanse of undecorated form in the place. In fact some visitors like Thackeray's Mr Molony thought they displayed a deal too much bare flesh:

> There's statues bright
> Of marble white,
> Of silver, and of copper;
> And some of zinc,
> And some, I think,
> That isn't over proper.

10. Sportsman's knife with eighty blades and instruments, by J. Rodgers & Sons. London 1851.

In a society in which even a table leg bare of cloth or other decoration was an unusual sight, voluptuous statues were indeed a surprise. Victorians did not talk publicly about such things, and yet here were these statues, often coyly hiding themselves seductively behind thinly sculptured veils in the best traditions of modern 'girlie' magazines.

There were also clothed statues, amongst them Thomas and Mary Thornycroft's baroque-style equestrian statue of Queen Victoria. But it was Augustus Kiss's *Amazon* cast in zinc, the famous *Greek Slave* by Hiram Powers in the American section and perhaps most sensational of all, *Dorothea from Don Quixote* by John Bell (which also appeared on a gas bracket designed by Henry Cole under his pseudonym of Felix Summerly), that created most comment: 'it may be safely said that the artist incurs an amazing risk in combining the half nude with positively frilled garments.' (8)

Perhaps one of the most thrilling sections was the moving machinery section where the recently invented mass-production machines of the industrial revolution were hard at work planning, slotting, drilling, boring, riveting, wire-drawing, spinning, coining and pumping, powered by steam from the specially built boiler house outside the exhibition. Even the machinery had overtones of the Victorian craze for historic design and there were engines in the Egyptian and Gothic styles on show.

The theme of one section of the exhibition was entirely medieval, with furniture, hangings, vessels and even books all conforming to the same decorative style. The whole was arranged by Augustus Pugin in the form of a 'medieval court', which some thought displayed 'the taste and art of dead men'.

But it was to the international displays that the visitors were drawn having been suitably impressed by the British achievements. Here were to be found exotic and beautiful things from the Near and Far East, from Europe, from North America and from the British Colonies. Exhibits ranged from the extensive displays from France to the extraordinary selection of goods sent from America which included Colt revolvers, a case of 'cheap American Newspapers', a model of Niagara Falls, the Goodyear Vulcanised India Rubber Trophy, false teeth, and an 'intolerable deal of starred-and-striped banners and pasteboard effigies of eagles with outspread wings,' to say nothing of the *Greek Slave* and the much admired agricultural machinery. Although some visitors, like Sir Arthur Hallam Elton's children from Somerset, were disappointed because 'few marked foreigners were distinguishable' most visitors, like one from Nottingham, could hardly describe the effect of the whole enterprise they were so overcome by it all:

What a sight is there! Neither pen nor pencil can portray it; language fails to give an adequate description of it. A Palace of iron and glass of astonishing magnitude, such as the world has never witnessed before, and may be styled one of the wonders of the world . . . I was astonished at the outside of the building, but when I entered at the door of the south transept I beheld a sight which absolutely bewildered me. The best productions of art and science of almost all lands in the civilised world lay before me. I gazed with astonishment. I knew not what direction to take. (9)

The overall effect must have been overwhelming especially when one considers that a great number of the visitors had not seen London or even a large city before. 165,000 visitors could thank Thomas Cook's Midland Railway excursions for the opportunity to visit the Crystal Palace. They were provided with their train and entrance tickets as well as a free copy of *Cook's Exhibition Herald and Excursion Organiser* weekly which pointed out, amongst other things, the features of the railway journey to London and gave details of 'suitable' temperance hotels like Lloyd's and Angus's. It was such excursions along with the special 'shilling days' that gave many more people a chance to see this great international gathering.

6,039,195 visitors had seen the exhibition by the time it closed on 11 October 1851, a daily average of almost 43,000 people. They had consumed 1,092,337 bottles of soft drinks, 934,691 baths buns and 870,027 plain buns but no alcohol which Mr Thomas Cook, amongst others, would have been pleased to note was not on sale. Dogs and smoking were also banned.

22

11. Chair by M. August Kitschett of Vienna: 'more remarkable for the taste of the upholsterer than the wood-carver'. London 1851. (*Art Journal*, 1851)

That the exhibition was a success was never in doubt and after the accountants had finished their work they announced a profit of £186,437. After much discussion it was decided to use most of the surplus – after giving an award of £5,000 to Paxton – for educational purposes and particularly the purchase of 87 acres of land at South Kensington as a site for a centre for arts and sciences. Today this site houses, among others, the Victoria and Albert, Science and Geological Museums, the Royal Albert Hall, the Imperial College of Science and Technology, and the Royal Colleges of Art and Music. It also provided the sites for the 1862 International Exhibition (where today the British Museum of Natural History stands) and the 1886 Colonial and Indian Exhibition. Bursaries were also provided in the arts and sciences, and scholarships which continue to be operated by the Royal Commission for the Exhibition of 1851 from their offices off Exhibition Road. These have to date produced 119 Fellows of the Royal Society and eight Nobel Laureates.

Other benefits included reformation of the patent and design protection laws and improved international communications. The Crystal Palace itself had been so admired that many people wanted to turn it into a winter garden and leave it in Hyde Park. The Commissioners, however, were committed to removing it and so, apart from its foundations which still lie beneath the turf of Hyde Park, it was dismantled and re-erected at Sydenham in South London in a much enlarged version where it was opened to the public by Queen Victoria on 10 June 1854. It lasted as London's Play Centre for 82 years through various financial crises, and was the scene of a great Festival of Empire in 1911, the year of King George V's Coronation.

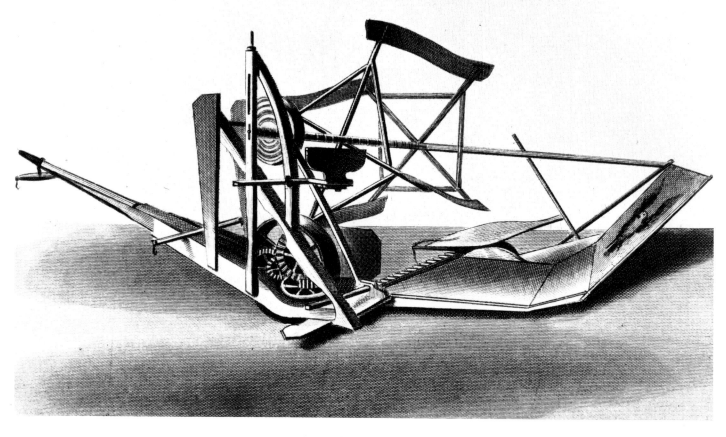

12. McCormick's American reaping machine. London 1851. (*Tallis's History and Description of the Crystal Palace . . . 1851*)

At six o'clock on the evening of 30 November 1936 a fire was discovered in a staff lavatory in the central transept. So much wood – 65,000 tons in all – had been used in the construction that the fire raced through it and within half-an-hour the whole building was alight. By the following morning nothing remained but a tangle of twisted metal and molten glass with the two great water-towers standing sentry over all.

Today the site with its gardens and waterworks laid out by Paxton is a wilderness. Some of it has been given over to a National Sports Centre and the building foundations support the BBC's television transmitter. But all attempts to turn it into a national exhibition centre once more have failed.

CHAPTER THREE

The Copyists, The First Paris 'Exposition Universelle' and London Again

Went to the Exhibition, where I noticed the fountain that sprouts artificial flowers.
I think all these machines are very depressing. I hate these contrivances that look as though they
are producing remarkable effects entirely on their own volition.

Delacroix, 1855 (trans. Norton)

If the proverb writer is to be believed, imitation is the sincerest flattery, and the 1851 exhibition was not immune. The basic idea of an exhibition that was international in scope was not the only thing to be copied, and Paxton's concept of a modular building was reproduced in varying forms at many subsequent shows from national and international to purely local. Unfortunately few of the copies met with the same success as the original. Repetition, often on a smaller scale, and without major alteration or evolution was not enough to ensure automatic success. Neither did the copyists have royal patronage and involvement, a site in the centre of the world's major city nor the uniqueness of the 1851 project.

In May 1834 the Royal Dublin Society had opened the first in a series of triennial exhibitions along the lines of the French National Exhibitions and although the seventh exhibition in the series had officially been restricted to Irish exhibitors, like its predecessors, some exhibits from England and Scotland had been allowed in. 1853 had been selected for the eighth and latest of these Irish National Exhibitions of Manufactures, and following the example set in 1851 at least two men began to consider the possibility of increasing the scope of the proposed Dublin Exhibition of 1853.

William Dargan who had trained as a surveyor and worked with Thomas Telford had pursued a career which involved him in almost every Irish railway and canal undertaking and made him a rich man. Unlike many Victorian engineers and entrepreneurs, he was a quiet, retiring man who did not actively encourage publicity. The 1851 exhibition had so impressed him as an exercise in peaceful international co-operation, that Dargan offered to put up £20,000 towards the costs and required no return, unless the project made a profit. He asked for the Society's own garden to be used as the site, and for Cusack Patrick Roney, a successful railway official, who was already well known in England as a highly competent organizer, to be made Secretary of the undertaking. Roney agreed on the condition that he was unpaid, honorary, Secretary. So the project started life with a large bank balance, the services of a qualified organizer and the very minimum of conditions imposed on it by Dargan.

Roney immediately commenced work by visiting as many European capitals as he could and persuading the governments concerned to send exhibits, thereby increasing the scope of the exhibition far beyond Dargan's intention of opening it to 'the three Kingdoms' of Britain. Meanwhile, an assistant secretary, John C. Deane, had been appointed and he visited English, Scottish and Welsh manufacturers with the same purpose. Since it had been decided that the exhibition should include a Fine Art Court, Deane concentrated particularly on the collection of art exhibits. One of the prime acquisitions was the superb collection of Indian and Oriental artifacts which had been collected by the East India Company for the Crystal Palace Exhibition. It had subsequently become an embarrassment to the 1851 Commissioners as the Company neither wanted the collection broken up nor returned to them. The Irish organizers heard of the problem and wasted no time in offering free space which provided them with splendid exhibits and much free publicity. The Japanese material was of particular interest, as it gave many people their first view of Japanese arts and crafts just a few years before America's Commodore Perry finally forced Japan into trade with the West.

13. Great Exhibition Building, Dublin 1853.

The energy of Roney and Deane resulted in an almost daily increase in the scope of the exhibition, such was the overwhelming response to their efforts. As a result more money had to be found and Dargan gave an additional £6,000 followed soon after by £14,000 more, making his total individual financial support £40,000.

Meanwhile a competition, with a first prize of £50, had been held to find a suitable building design and was won by John Benson, a civil engineer who had also been responsible for the design of the 1852 Cork Exhibition Building. Like the Crystal Palace, the building was supported by a modular cast iron and wood frame of columns and girders, but only a small portion of the roof was glazed, the remainder being clad in wood with a covering of paper, canvas and tar which was then lime washed. The original design had three galleries: one large central gallery and two smaller side aisles, but the increase in exhibits meant that two additional galleries had to be built. The resulting complex was described by one critic as 'five Brobdignagian vegetable marrows laid side by side'!

The erection of the huge laminated wood ribs for the main hall of the building caused great trouble. Although structurally sound, once installed and cross-tied by purlins, they had individually virtually no lateral strength at all. 25 feet wider than the 1851 ribs, they

26

whipped alarmingly 'like gigantic fishing rods' (1) and the first rib nearly collapsed under its own weight. Added to this, the six months' schedule for construction of the buildings was nearly upset completely when the entire roof of the southern hall was destroyed by a storm on Christmas morning 1852.

As well as causing building problems, Benson's design was criticized for being too dark inside. One of the drawbacks of Paxton's Crystal Palace had been the enormous amount of light it let into the interior. Special blinds had been fitted to certain areas of the building to help cut down the level of light and some sections, like the music and lace exhibits, had been tented over. However when the 1853 exhibition opened the critics saw that their fears were unfounded for although it was not as bright inside as the Crystal Palace, and there were even dark corners on dull days, 'by the use of a fluted and greenish-coloured glass a delicious quality of light has been secured – a cool, greyish tone prevails, and there is an utter absence of direct rays of sunshine; so that exhibitors of pictures and of fabrics may be assured that however delicate the colouring may be, there is a fair prospect of objects leaving the Exhibition as bright and pure in their tints as when they were first deposited there'. (2) Indeed because of the gentle overhead lighting almost all the critics commended the building for the way in which the fine art was displayed. It was considered to be an excellent solution to a problem which still exercises art gallery designers and critics today.

Roney and Deane's enthusiasm unfortunately resulted in the entire project being above the head of the average Irish visitor who viewed it with much the same uneducated eye as people 'up from the country' had viewed 1851. Although the editors of the *Art Journal* catalogue of the exhibition believed that 'this exhibition will contribute very largely to render Ireland that which she is so eminently qualified to become – a manufacturing country' the fact of the matter became clear to them by the time they came to write the introduction to their 1855 Paris Exposition catalogue. 'As a means of encouraging and developing Irish industry it was simply absurd ... and the Dublin experiment was to Hibernian industry what a dress coat and white kid gloves would be to the shirtless, shoeless, and bare-headed "gossoon"!' In fact until the ridiculously high entry charge of 5/– was reduced in the middle of June, very few members of the general public could even afford to visit the exhibition.

Dargan was the recipient of 'universal praise and thanks' but he was not decorated and possibly lived to regret his generosity for the Exhibition lost nearly £20,000.

One memorial to Dargan remains. Following the success of the fine art loan section of the exhibition it was decided to set up an Irish National Gallery in 1854 which today houses one of the great collections of Europe. This gallery was built in part as a tribute to Dargan and to this day his statue stands in front of it.

The 1851 exhibition and particularly its building had also greatly impressed the Americans who had seen it. One of them, Horace Greeley, noted on his return home that 'the Crystal Palace, which covers and protects all, is better than any one thing in it.' Another, Edward Riddle, returned to New York and contacted P. T. Barnum, the circus owner and showman, and tried to interest him in the idea of holding such an event in America. He failed, but he did manage to interest some of New York's merchants and bankers in the project and on 3 January 1852 the Corporation of the City of New York granted them a five year lease, at a peppercorn rent of one dollar per annum, on Reservoir Square (now Bryant Square) on two conditions: 'first, that the building should be composed of iron and glass; and secondly, that no single entrance-charge should exceed fifty cents'.

The American Secretary of State agreed to classify the building as a bonded warehouse and contacted foreign nations on its behalf, and it had a virtually free site, but the exhibition suffered from inter-State jealousies and no official government backing. 'The Association for the Exhibition of the Industry of All Nations' was just as high minded and keen to succeed as London's 1851 Commission but it had little chance of success in the not-so-United States of America of 1853.

Once again an international competition was organized for the design of the building.

14. Clock by M. Paillard of Paris: 'it is not overcharged with ornament, but combines solidity with grace and richness'. Dublin 1853. (*Art Journal*, 1853)

15. Revolving pistol by Colonel Sam Colt of New York and London. Dublin 1853. (*Art Journal*, 1853)

16. A 'metallic bedstead . . . of peculiar excellence' by R. W. Winfield of Birmingham. Dublin 1853. (*Art Journal*, 1853)

17. New York 1853 – the interior showing the central dome and George Washington's statue beneath.

18. New York in 1853 looking south from 42nd street. Crystal Palace and Reservoir in the foreground.

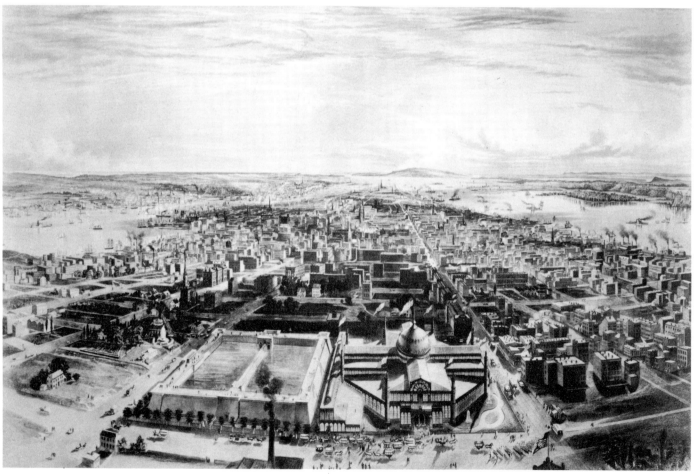

Paxton was one of the many architects and engineers who submitted entries but his design did not fit into the site. Some of the plans were exceedingly daring: the one submitted by Hamilton Hoppin and James Bogardus (one of the first architects to evolve our present-day system of metal frame construction with curtain walling between) had a roof suspended by chains from a central 300 foot high cast-iron circular tower. The building committee, however, chose a much more mundane design by Charles Gildemeister and his partner, George Carstensen, who had been responsible for the layout of the famous Tivoli Gardens in his native Copenhagen. Its structural system was almost identical to London's Crystal Palace although the form was dictated by the square site. The roof was clad in white pine boards and tinned, and the interior was illuminated through the glass walls and clerestory windows in the main avenues and dome.

The interior decoration by Henry Greenough used pastel tones with the structural detail picked out in primary and secondary colours and gold. Signor Monte Lilla designed the interior of the dome, facing it with tempora painted canvas pierced by thirty-two coloured stained glass windows showing the arms of the Union and the several States. With grand staircases at each corner below the dome and a large equestrian statue of Washington by Baron Marochetti (the largest exhibit in the show), the building was a suitably impressive centrepiece to the whole exhibition. Gas lighting was supplied for policing and cleaning purposes and towards the end of the exhibition's run the building was opened on certain evenings when 'the effect of the interior, when fully illuminated, especially the dome, was exceedingly grand'. (3) Unfortunately, however, the roof leaked at the beginning, and many visitors and exhibits got wet when it rained.

Structurally much more interesting was *Latting's Observatory and Ice-Cream Parlour* which was built by a New York businessman opposite the palace. Above the ice-cream

19. Elisha Graves Otis demonstrating his patent lift. New York 1853. (Otis Elevator Company, New York)

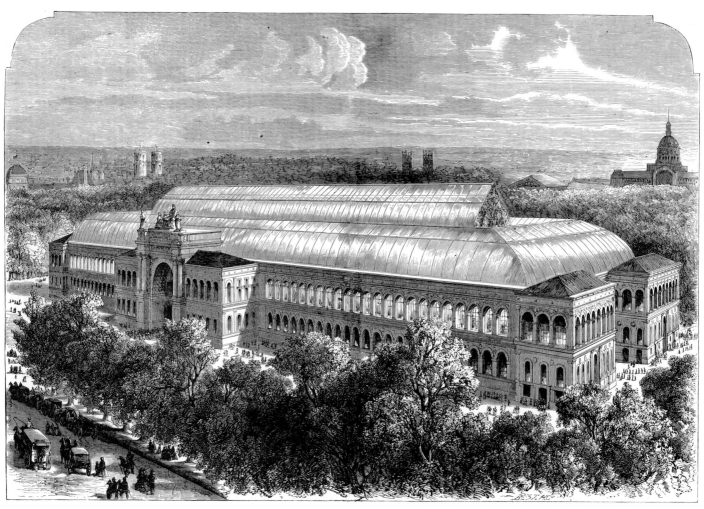

20. View from the Champs-Elysées of the 1855 Palais de l'Industrie. (*L'Illustration, Journal Universal*, 1854)

parlour was a viewing platform which was reached by an 'often balky steam elevator'. One of the more spectacular exhibits in the palace itself was Elisha Grave Otis' 'safety elevator'. He gave personal demonstrations by mounting the platform, being hauled aloft and ordering the rope to be cut. As the weight of the lift on the springs released the safety dogs and they latched into the ratchet bars on the guide rails securing the platform, Mr Otis would remove his hat with a flourish, bow and exclaim, 'All safe, gentlemen, all safe', whilst the visitors roared their approval.

The Palace was opened three months late on 14 July 1853 by President Franklin Pierce who was one of the first of many to see the exhibition as a possible means of welding the States of America together once more. Very few Americans had been able to visit the 1851 Exhibition, and the New York building had as great a local effect as the Crystal Palace had had on the English crowds three years before:

> . . . A Palace,
> Lofter, fairer, ampler than any yet,
> Earth's modern wonder, History's Seven
> out stripping,
> High rising tier on tier, with glass and
> iron façades,
> Gladdening the sun and sky – enhued in
> cheerfullest hues,
> Bronze, lilac, robin's-egg, marine and crimson,
> Over whose golden roof shall flaunt, beneath
> thy banner, Freedom. (4)

Despite the variety of exhibits, the project failed to make money from the start, and by the end of 1853 it was well over $100,000 in debt. Once again Barnum was approached, and for four months he tried everything in his repertoire of attractions to resolve the loss. But even he was beaten, and he resigned on 10 July 1854. The Association struggled on but by the close of the exhibition on 1 November 1854 the final debt had risen to over $300,000.

For the next two years the building was used for fairs and functions and then reverted, via the Official Receiver, to the City of New York. Five months later, during the American Institute's annual fair the building caught fire and despite the 21 million gallons of water in the adjoining reservoir, burnt to the ground within half-an-hour. 'So bursts a bubble rather noteworthy in the annals of New York. To be accurate, the bubble burst some years ago, and this catastrophe merely annihilates the apparatus that generated it.' (5)

On the other side of the Atlantic the French had begun to plan a huge international exhibition. The newly named Paris Exposition Universelle was scheduled for 1855. It was not a good year for such an event. There was still fighting in the Crimea, and for an exhibition that claimed to be 'a temple of peace, bringing all nations together in concord', this was unfortunate to say the least. Few advances had been made in the four years since 1851, and the project mirrored the British exhibition a little too closely to give Paris the element of surprise and innovation so much a part of the magic and wonder of London's Crystal Palace. But it was an object of civic pride and a successful national public relations exercise. It was financed by the French Government, and Napoleon III had added prestige and his personal backing by appointing his cousin Prince Napoleon as the Chief Administrator.

A permanent exhibition hall, the Palais de l'Industrie, was constructed alongside that favourite meeting place of fashionable Second Empire Paris, the Champs Elysées. Manufacturers and the press were at first slow to show any interest but as the opening day came nearer the demand for space and publicity increased enormously. The interior was soon filled, as were the additional temporary extensions. A rotunda which had been built earlier in the gardens of the Champs Elysées, was used to show the French crown jewels and valuable carpets and tapestries, the Palais des Beaux-Arts was built on the Avenue Montaigne to house the Fine Arts, and the exhibits in the Machinery Gallery gradually stretched to cover three quarters of a mile along the banks of the Seine. This kind of poor planning, and the absence of one central building led to great diffusion of effort and lack of cohesion in the exhibition.

The Palais de l'Industrie had been authorized by the Emperor in March 1852 but it was not until February 1854 that work begun in earnest, and when the exhibition finally opened two weeks late, it was still unfinished and reminded many cynical Parisians of theatres 'where the curtain goes up on actors en deshabillé'.

The Palais was 'A rectangular building, covering eight acres of ground ... the main exhibition hall being spanned by a central arched roof ... with two side arches parallel to the centre one; and two of the same span running transversely at the ends, and beyond its gables. At the corners these latter connected by hips and ridges, leaving a clear space

21. 'Detail of scroll panel by MM Huber Frères of Paris in gold on a white ground'. Paris 1855. (*Art Journal*, 1855)

22. Cabinet by M. Audot of Paris: 'the bold and elegantly turned sweeps of which the design is composed . . . are nowhere broken by injudicious projecting ornaments.' Paris 1855. (*Art Journal*, 1855)

23. Display of products from the French Colonies. Paris 1855. (*L'Illustration, Journal Universel*, 1855)

underneath. The covering of a large portion of these roofs (about one-third) was roughened glass, which, together with great defects in ventilation (there were none of the louvre panels of Paxton's 1851 building) appears to have been a serious mistake in the hot summer climate of Paris – great inconvenience being experienced in consequence, and it being necessary to resort to the expedient of muslin screens'. (6) The wide spans and the lightness of the iron construction successfully carried the roof only with the help of enormous and expensive blocks of lead which were used as abutments and saved the necessity of using buttresses. It was an unusual building to say the least and was described by one critic as 'a crystal palace hidden in an envelope of stone'. Another tried to analyse its failures: 'Nowhere was the internal arrangement of the building expressed or even suggested on the outside, and the consequence was that, however beautiful either of the parts might be separately, the design was a failure as a whole'. (7) Nevertheless this cocooning of a glass structure within a decorative stone facing was to be copied by exhibition hall designers well into the twentieth century and even today can be seen in the surviving halls of Olympia in London and the Grand Palais in Paris. The Palais de l'Industrie was to remain on the site serving its original purpose until 1897 when it was demolished to make way for the buildings of the 1900 Exposition. If the main exhibition building was considered generally inferior to the Crystal Palace, in one element at least the French did have the edge over the British Exhibition. Despite the efforts of such bodies as the Society of Arts and individuals like Henry Cole in their promotion of Art in manufacture, the British had found it difficult to weld together what they still saw as two different fields of endeavour – Fine Art and Industry. Indeed Fine Arts as such had been left out of the exhibit listing of

1851 except as examples of manufacturers' skills. Art exhibitions had, in fact, developed earlier in Britain, but they had been divorced from the subsequent development of the industrial exhibition.

In France the demarcation line between Fine Art and Industry had never been drawn so strongly and indeed the first French National Exhibition had exhibited the fine art-based industries of Sèvres, Gobelins and Savonneries. In his official announcement of plans for the 1855 Exposition Universelle, Louis Napoleon, Napoleon III since 1852, stated that arts were as important as industry, and so they were automatically included, and in many ways the Palais des Beaux-Arts became the most important section of the exhibition. The hanging space had been greatly increased by the use of floor-mounted screens. It was lit by means of roof-lights with an internal ceiling of translucent glass which further mellowed the light and also allowed proper ventilation in the roof without danger to the paintings from rainwater and leakage. It was expected that French artists would dominate the display there, although Charles Baudelaire, the French critic, remarked that the 'English section of the exhibition is very fine, most uncommonly fine, and worthy of a long and patient study'. He was particularly impressed with the work of Britain's Pre-Raphaelites. The two most popular French artists were Ingres and Delacroix, and competition between them inspired caricatures and cartoons in the French press. Each had his critics and loyal supporters who went to quite blatant lengths in their criticisms of the opposition: 'For a number of years the whole glory of the French school seemed to be concentrated in a single man – and I certainly do not mean M. Ingres'. (8)

A new system of classification of the exhibits for the Exposition Universelle was evolved by the great French engineer Frédéric Le Play, 'one of the freshest minds of the century'. Like the method suggested by Prince Albert in 1851, the scheme had high intellectual motives but was completely impractical: 'The classification adopted on paper has resulted in a most glorious defiance of almost everything like classification in the actual arrangements. Not content with a *single* intelligible principle, its authors adopted *two*. In one, objects are classified according to use, in the other according to the nature of the material, or mode of manufacture'. (9) Nevertheless, in one section of the exhibition could be found the beginnings of today's thematic exhibits. Originally suggested by Thomas Twining, a member of the Council of the London Society of Arts, it consisted of a 'Special collecting of articles of domestic and sanitary economy for the use of the working classes'. Emperor Napoleon duly formed a special commission to undertake 'to select throughout the whole exhibition such articles as their cheapness, combined with good quality, may render particularly useful in a simple home' rather than the grand, glorious and highly expensive Second Empire display pieces found in most sections of the exhibition. Although this *Exposition Economique* opened almost two months after the rest of the show it proved very popular.

For the first time the British Government had given financial support to the British exhibitors, most of whom were hoping that their interest and active participation in the Exposition would encourage the French to simplify and lower the complicated Anglo-French trade barriers. Although this did not happen, general Anglo-French relations were improved with the visit of Queen Victoria and Prince Albert to Paris and the exhibition at the invitation of the Emperor. The Queen was the first reigning British monarch to set foot on French soil since Henry V, 400 years earlier.

The French attitude to finance was very different from the British one and they even allowed prices to appear on the exhibits, an action which struck one pompous English critic as reducing the whole exhibition to the level of an 'immense bazaar'. Unlike the British exhibitions which were originated and financed by private enterprise, the project was financed by the French Government which for the first time, and much to the disgust of the French population, instigated an entrance charge. Nevertheless, although the total attendance figures were far in excess of those from the previous French National Exhibition in 1849, the entire project made a staggering loss of over eight million francs.

Prince Napoleon's report, far from glossing over the problems, criticized the direct government support, the exhibition planning and the complete lack of impartiality of the

END

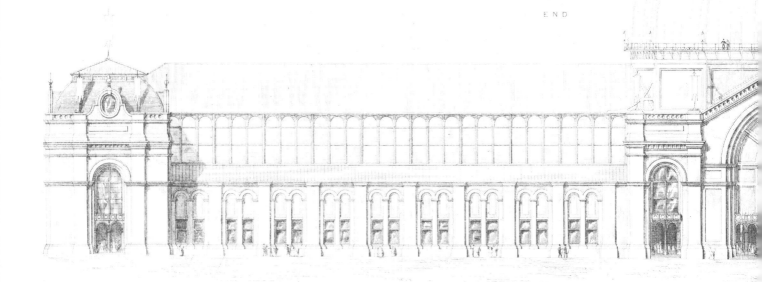

24. Elevations of the 1862 London International Exhibition.

judging which meant that many of the awards were given for political reasons. He also suggested that the days of the great Universal Exhibitions were numbered and that special exhibitions, dealing with one particular subject only, should replace them.

However the first Exposition Universelle had been a triumphant demonstration of the aspirations of the Second Empire for peace and progress, and of pride in the beginnings of positive achievement, although it made a loss in financial terms.

Meanwhile Britain was planning a sequel to 1851. Once again the Society of Arts was the instigating body, and because of the terrific success of 1851 it experienced no difficulty in finding support for its proposals. The 1851 Commissioners were approached and agreed to make available some of their South Kensington land rent free. A new Royal Commission

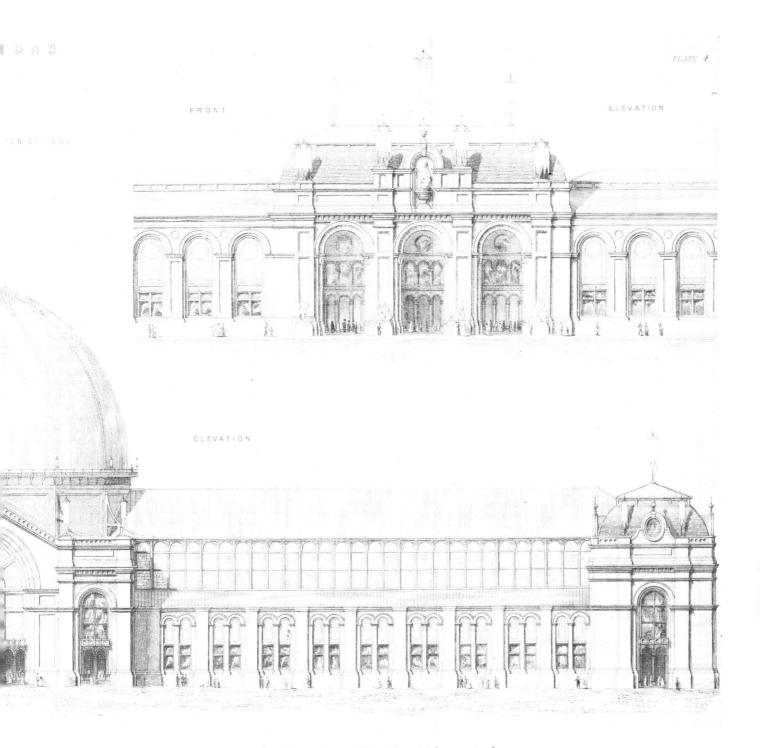

FRONT ELEVATION

ELEVATION

was formed and Henry Cole took on the job of 'Consulting Officer', in which capacity he was able to supply most of the necessary experience and direction for the work. The ease with which the organization proceeded lulled the Commissioners into thinking they automatically had another 1851 success on their hands, and much committee time was wasted deciding what they were to do with the profits they so confidently expected. They would have done well to have remembered the fate of some of the exhibitions held since 1851.

Cole was responsible for the choice of a building design by Captain Fowkes of the Royal Engineers, who had been secretary to the British Department at the 1855 Paris Exposition Universelle. It was a building which the *Art Journal* considered a 'wretched shed'

25. 'Gwynne & Co.'s double-acting centrifugal pump, worked by a pair of their horizontal steam engines'. (*The Illustrated Record of the International Exhibition*, 1862)

compared with Paxton's Crystal Palace, and was almost universally condemned as ugly and featureless except for its twin domes. Built on Cromwell Road where the British Museum (Natural History) stands today, the building appeared far too large for the site, covering nearly all of it and making it impossible to view the overall front elevation except from a very oblique angle. The architectural and engineering professions did not bother to stem their jealousies and disappointments either. In fact it was intended that the 'utilitarian structure', as the organizers quite openly called it, should have large coloured mosaic pictures applied to the bare panels of the outside walls. Each panel was to represent a main exhibit category – the leading British artists of the day, amongst them Holman Hunt, Leighton, Millais, Rossetti, Cope and Mulready, had already been picked for the work and experiments were in hand to produce the finished mosaics. In the event they never materialised and the building was demolished soon after the end of the exhibition, much to most people's relief.

The exhibition was larger in area inside than the Crystal Palace, although not so big as the 1855 Paris exhibition, and it included a fine art section. In his article in the official catalogue John Hollingshead summed up the character of the period:

We may not be more moral, more imaginative, nor better educated than our ancestors, but we have steam, gas, railways and power looms, while there are more of us and we have more money to spend.

It was the time of the height of Victorian design and the strength of the 1862 exhibition lay in its exhibits. Since 1851 there had been advances in the manufacturing techniques,

38

technical application and invention first seen by the general public at the Crystal Palace. Aniline dyes, the first discovery in a branch of chemistry which supplies many items of our modern way of life, were in production following Bechamp's distillation of Aniline from Benzine in 1856. Photography too had developed apace as the photographs of the exhibition by the London Stereographic Company illustrate. The use of steam power, particularly in agriculture, had increased enormously, and the communications field had raced ahead with the use of the electric telegraph, marine cables and the repeal of paper duties, while printing techniques had developed rapidly. The soap tax had also been repealed and Mr William Hawes, the Registrar General, could report that 'the people are better employed, crime is decreasing, and their social and intellectual condition is improved'.

The furniture designed by William Morris and exhibited by his firm, Messrs Morris, Marshall & Faulkner & Company: Fine Art Workmen in Painting, Carving, Furniture and the Metals (formed by Morris in 1861 with support from his Pre-Raphaelite friends),

27. Souvenir toilet soap packaging. London 1862 (Unilever, London)

26. Bennett's display: The time ball fell every hour down the face of the fluted column. London 1862. (*Cassell's Illustrated Exhibitor . . .*, 1862)

39

showed the first glimmerings of the arts and crafts movement away from the existing high Victorian style with its elaborate furnishings and liberal applications of pattern and texture to every available face of every article. Other furniture was designed by Rossetti and Philip Webb, and there was a whole range of 'medieval' wooden furniture and examples of the influence of the Gothic revival and medieval art on the members of the Ecclesiological Society, showing their work for the first time in public alongside the Pre-Raphaelite Brotherhood. The development of the aesthetic movement in Britain was stimulated by some of the foreign displays at the exhibition. The Japanese exhibits aroused the enthusiasm of, among others, Arthur Liberty. His company, Liberty's of Regent Street, came to lead the oriental movement by the end of the nineteenth century. The foreign exhibits in all sections far out-shone those of the 1851 Exhibition with France once more leading the field. The Americans were badly represented again, because of the disorder caused by the American Civil War which also prevented any official American presence.

At the end of the central nave, in front of the 38ft 5in. diameter clock made by Dent's, was a gold obelisk nearly 70ft in height. This was Victoria's Gold Trophy, erected to show the massive volume of 800 tons, 17cwt, 3qtrs and 7lbs of gold sent from the Australian colony to Britain in the ten years from 1851 to 1861. 'We had in this attractive object one of the most skilful applications of simple materials for the production of a very satisfactory result; these materials being only wooden poles, canvas and gold leaf; while the whole

28. The Hereford Cathedral Screen by Skidmore's Art Manufacturing Company, Coventry. London 1862. (J. B. Waring *Masterpieces of Industrial Art and Sculpture . . .*, 1862)

effect produced was that of an enormous mass of bullion' (10) – in short an early piece of exhibition display!

Once again there were many special excursions to London to the exhibition, although the Midlands Railway refused to allow Thomas Cook to run his excursions as before – he had made too great a percentage on each ticket in 1851! However because of the national shock caused by the death of Prince Albert from typhoid only four and a half months earlier, the wettest summer weather for years and the lack of public opposition ('Oh for the opposition of 1851, that's a stimulant wanting now!'), as well as the lack of a symbolic masterpiece like Paxton's Crystal Palace, the exhibition never really caught the public imagination, and today is almost forgotten – so much so that when the Victoria and Albert Museum, of which Henry Cole had been the first Director, held a commemorative exhibition in 1962, one London newspaper headed an article 'The Forgotten Exhibition'. Contrary to the general expectations of the Commissioners the exhibition made a loss and the guarantors were only saved by the generosity of Sir John Kelk, a partner in one of the building's joint main contractors, Messrs Lucas and Messrs Kelk. Not only did they agree to take on both the permanent and temporary building materials to help offset their outstanding accounts, but Sir John also personally donated the sum of £11,000 to enable the books to balance.

Today this clearing of debts and even, as in the case of Dublin in 1853, complete financing of an international exhibition with little obvious material return, seems extraordinary. To the Victorians, with their high ideals and philanthropic approach to life and learning, especially amongst the highly literate new upper-middle classes, nothing could have been more satisfactory as a way of caring for the less fortunate members of the population.

29. The Japanese Court. London 1862.
(*Illustrated London News*, 1862)

The Big Step Forward and the American Centennial Exposition

> I believe my children will learn more of the condition of the arts, agriculture, customs, manufactures and mineral and vegetable products of the world in five weeks than they could by books at home in five years, and as many years' travel.
>
> *Samuel Morse (American) 1867*

Only six months after the close of the London exhibition Napoleon III announced that France would be holding the second of her Expositions Universelles in Paris in 1867. The French had realized that an increase in size would not guarantee the success of an international exhibition – a truth illustrated only too clearly by the 1862 London exhibition. The 1867 exposition included many new features which today form an important part of any international exhibition – national pavilions and restaurants, an amusement park, special gardens and waterways, and perhaps most important of all, the beginnings of culturally based thematic display techniques.

The classification of exhibits was based on the system used in 1855 but with the added sophistication of arrangement by country of origin as well as by classified type –

manufactures, and products of cognate natures, to be arranged in concentric bands, with a garden in the middle. The different nationalities to intersect the bands by transepts or avenues radiating from the centre. (1)

The idea for this classification scheme can be traced back to an article that appeared in the English periodical *The Builder* on 16 February 1861 by George Maw and illustrated by a theoretical building design by the Birmingham architect, Edward Payne. Maw and Payne had hoped to influence the organizers of the 1862 London exhibition with their scheme but the lateness of their publication had ruled out any chance of this. The faults of the system

30. Plan of the 1867 Paris Exposition layout – the American translator's French was not too good : the central section was an exhibition on the history of work (*travail*) not 'travel'. (*Harper's Bazaar*, 1867)

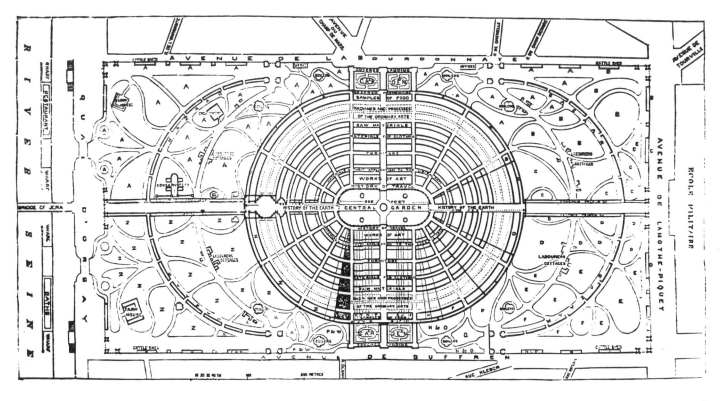

became apparent when it was realized that not all countries could produce sufficient material in all the major categories. Some, like the large industrial nations of Europe, had a large quantity of manufactured goods and little or no raw materials, whilst those with predominantly agrarian economies such as the lands of the Near East, had only produce and raw materials to show, with little if anything in the way of engineering or manufactures.

The oblong site on the Champ de Mars, used for the first French National Exhibition sixty-nine years before, had already necessitated a change in the shape of the exhibition building from circular to elliptical. Next the varying sizes of the categories destroyed the planned orderly layout and almost defeated the whole object of the building's design. Nevertheless, it is interesting to note that Barcelona's first 'exposición internacional de 1888', which took place on the site of today's Parque de la Ciudadela, also used this idea, on a much smaller scale, with a semi-circular building.

Victor Hugo wrote the introduction to *Lacroix' Paris-Guide* for the exhibition in the form of a manifesto 'To the Peoples of Europe' and the entire venture was carried through on a high intellectual plane which reflected the whole exotic lifestyle of Second Empire Paris with its flowery language and decoration: 'To make a circuit of this place, circular, like the equator, is literally to go around the world. All peoples are here, enemies live in peace side by side. As in the beginning of things, on the globe of waters, the divine spirit now floats on this globe of iron.' Visitors like Henry Adams remained un-impressed however, at least by the intellectual standards of the visitors:

I did not detect a single refined-looking being . . . but there may have been one or two who, like ourselves, had drifted there by accident or necessity.

Although the Emperor had appointed Prince Napoleon as overall controller, he made Frédéric le Play, an engineer, economist and acknowledged expert on European labour conditions, the Director of the exhibition and gave him responsibility for the layout and general organization. The exhibition building was ringed with concentric galleries around a central garden and le Play suggested that the first of these should be used for 'L'Histoire du Travail'. This exhibit, with its theme of the history of work, was the first attempt at an international thematic display, a facet of future international exhibitions which was to reach its peak one hundred years later in Montreal at Expo '67. The display showed the various phases through which each country had passed before arriving at its present state of civilization, and was intended as a preface to the entire exhibition. Indeed, it was hoped that it would place the new inventions and endeavours in the remainder of the building in their true historical perspective. The French section, with a complete survey from the Stone Age to the Eighteenth Century, was easily the best. Some countries, for instance Sweden which showed the cradle of King Charles XII, had what one chronicler called 'very curious articles'.

31. Handpainted glass slide of Paris showing the 1867 Exposition Building. (Science Museum, London)

32. 'The History of Work' retrospective display
– a selection of the exhibits in a graphic design
by M. Lancelot. Paris 1867. (*L'Exposition
Universelle de 1867 Illustrée*)

The Department of Art which occupied the next gallery provided the exhibition with a
great deal of publicity, not all of it good. Unlike the 1855 exhibition, the 1867 organizers
only accepted pictures which had been produced in the last twelve years and were
adamant in their refusal to allow some painters in at all. Some of the outlawed painters,
amongst them Pissaro, Cézanne, and Monet, accepted this but Manet and Courbet both
opened their own private galleries just outside the entrance to the exhibition grounds at
the end of the Pont de l'Alma. In fact it was while he was collecting the 50 centimes
entrance fees that Manet conceived his painting *Panorama of the Paris Exposition*.

Of those accepted for display, the European paintings were all heavily influenced by the
traditional French school, but the American and English paintings over which the selection

committee had little control, were 'quite different, showing much more character and individuality, the difference in the system of study throwing the artist entirely on his own resources and thereby bringing out his peculiar style, which, under the Continental method of teaching, might never develop'. (2)

The next corridor housed the Liberal Arts exhibits. Amongst these was a much admired display of surgical instruments and medical equipment, ranging from complete field hospitals to artificial limbs, from the Surgeon-General of the United States. The patented Rocking Chair, however, which was included in the American display, received more popular comment and acclaim. Furniture filled the next concentric gallery, along with other paraphernalia of the interior decoration of this extravagant period. There were pillars, gold statuettes, and inlaid metals and woods in profusion on all manner of items from desks to sideboards and from chairs to bedheads. Other pieces, like the Milton Shield made by Messrs Elkington's of London, demonstrated the superb craftsmanship of this period – a fact to be remembered even if the objects look ugly and over decorated to our eyes today.

Next to the Furniture was a Gallery of Textile Fabrics filled with gorgeous laces and embroideries on show alongside all the traditional weaving materials from the many countries taking part, like the cashmere shawls from India.

As a lead into the largest gallery there was a final smaller gallery displaying Raw Materials, covering all imaginable substances used in the processes of manufacturing. Many were shown in the still favoured form of 'trophies', such as the Prussian salt from Strassfurt which was cut into blocks and made into a half-dome rather like an igloo. Two new materials made their public bow. Petroleum, the cause of much injury and destruction in Paris only three years later, and aluminium, the new lightweight wonder metal discovered in 1754 but only refined in laboratory quantities in 1856. It was much admired by the Emperor who ordered a special dinner service made in what was then an extremely rare and precious metal.

The largest of the concentric galleries housed the Machinery. Here were vast numbers of manufactured articles arranged in trophies rising up on all sides, and 'a multitude of machines in motion, giving forth a thousand noises of all kinds, bewildering the mind and perplexing the ear'. Among the exhibits was a gigantic 50 ton Krupp steel cannon (everyone else still used bronze cannon) that fired 1,000lb. shells weighing in themselves more than most other cannon of the period – a sight that the French military men eyed with some interest following the Prussians' unexpectedly speedy defeat of the Austrians the year before. This display like others could be viewed from the raised balcony which ran down the centre of the section. Finally, on the seventh and outside ring were the exhibits of fresh and preserved foods with the highly popular national restaurants where 'visitors were waited upon by young girls in the costumes of the different nationalities, and one met the blondes of Bavaria, the gay Austrian, the pretty Russian, crowned with a tinsel diadem, the Mulatto offering cocoa and guava, Greeks, Swiss, Neapolitans, Italians, Indians, and even the Chinese women, with their little tea shop. All languages mingling strangely together on this promenade, and all nationalities elbowing each other, from the elegant Parisian to the Bedouin in his burnous.' (3)

The exhibition building was the first one to have the stresses and strains of its structure properly computed before its erection. This fact, and its careful detailing, owed much to its chief designer, Gustave Eiffel. It also overcame problems which the 1855 Palais de l'Industrie's lead blocks had failed to solve by having its structural roof support above roof level. The designers considered the projecting support members ugly, and flags and drapes were hung from them to give the impression that they were 'flag staves on the building itself, floating brilliant pennons, which gave a festive air to the whole scene and relieved the effect of the massive iron structure in a very agreeable manner'. (4) Inside, hydraulic lifts carried visitors from the ground floor to the roof and on to the *Promenoirs* or platforms which afforded splendid views out over the roof with its red arcades breached by the blue of the sky giving a sensation of the 'immensity of the Coliseum'.

But it was in the grounds surrounding the main building that many of the most visually

33. Three of the manufacturing demonstrations to be seen in the Exposition. Lacemaking by Lefébure et fils; Pipemaking by M. Cardon's craftsmen; Binoculars being made by M. Lemaire's craftsmen. (*L'Exposition Universelle de 1867 Illustrée*)

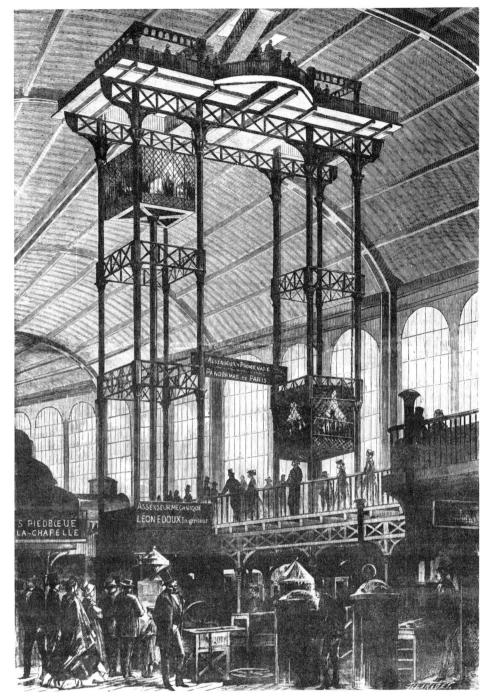

35. M. Léon Edoux's hydraulic lifts which took Exposition visitors up to the walkway on the roof of the main building. Paris 1867. (*L'Exposition Universelle de 1867 Illustrée*)

exciting things were to be found. For the first time at such an event, each participating country had been invited to erect its own individual buildings. The assortment of constructions that resulted gave the area the character of an enormous pleasure garden with the national architectural styles blending with the sideshows and the newly made gardens laid at great expense on the gravel parade ground of the Champ de Mars. There were a hundred and one small buildings, both educational and extraordinary, including mosques, Russian slobodas, Swiss châlets, Tunisian kiosks, Swedish cottages, English lighthouses, Egyptian palaces, stables for dromedaries, 'all massed in picturesque confusion'. 'The banners, the flames, the unfurled flags of the nations gave an impression of walking a street of the Middle Empire'. (5) One of these exhibits, the Tunisian Bardo, is still used in the Parc Montsouris in Paris as a meteorological observatory.

Opposite
34. The Spanish, Swedish, Austrian, Turkish and Chinese Cafés in the park surrounding the main Exposition building. Paris 1867. (*Illustrated London News 1867*)

Down on the banks of the River Seine there were models illustrating the history of naval construction and artillery. Visitors could take a sightseeing trip on the river itself in the Bateaux Mouches which were instigated for this exhibition and remain today an exceedingly popular Parisian tourist attraction. Nadar, the famous Parisian photographer, provided a more unusual view of events by taking twelve visitors at a time up in his double-decker captive balloon – the first time that the visitor had been able to have a live 'birds-eye-view' of an exhibition.

Despite the exhibition's success, there had been some bad moments. The very wet winter and the expectation that this, like all the previous Paris exhibitions, would open late or unfinished, had discouraged many from attending during the early weeks, and Thomas Cook's representative could still write a week after the official opening that 'there is nobody yet in Paris'. In fact the exhibition had opened on time after a tremendous clearing-up and finishing-off operation carried out by 500 extra workmen during the nine days preceding the official opening on 1 May 1867. But the Tsar of Russia was nearly assassinated in the Bois de Boulogne on the second day of his state visit to Paris, and Napoleon heard the first news of the assassination of Maximilian Schell in Mexico minutes before he left the Tuileries to drive to the Palais de l'Industrie for the distribution of the prizes and medals. There was also bad news of Garibaldi from Italy and reports of cholera and famine in Algeria. All the pomp and ceremony of the opening, with representatives from nearly all the royal families of Europe present and even Rossini's 'Hymn to the Emperor' composed specially for the occasion, could not conceal from some people the feeling that the Paris of 1867, with its surfeit of wine, women and song was just too good to last. Michel Chevalier, writing the official report, even expressed the fear that the exhibition would be 'like a meteor, bright but transient, in a horizon destined to become dark and stormy'. Less than three years later the Franco-Prussian war was indeed to prove it so.

In 1855 Prince Napoleon had suggested that the days of large scale international exhibitions were numbered, and that either permanent repositories or museums should be set up, or smaller shows restricted to a few exhibit categories should be held in their place. His ideas, which had been reiterated in a slightly different form by Frédéric le Play after the 1867 Exposition Universelle, caught the attention of Henry Cole who was particularly interested in the suggestion of a restricted range of categories of exhibits. He thought that a series of such shows over a period of a few years could cover the same ground as one large six month effort, that the exhibits could be more detailed and the same smaller buildings could house each year's selection of exhibits in succession. He enthusiastically approached the 1851 Commissioners who gave him permission to use land behind the newly built Albert Hall on their South Kensington site, and agreed to finance up to five one-year shows. The first of the London International Exhibitions was held in 1871 but unfortunately the whole series never really got off the ground. By its very nature, the exhibition only appealed to a certain sector of the population, and the method of classifying all the exhibits by subject made it impossible for the countries taking part to display their wares with all the local colour and showmanship so much a part of previous international exhibitions. The whole show became a dull, almost scientific, display of goods.

There were other reasons for the failure of the series. In 1871 the Franco-Prussian war was still being fought, although France managed to send over a series of items for exhibition. Then when the second exhibition (concerned with printing, paper, music and musical instruments, jewellery, cotton goods and fine arts) opened in 1872, the Royal Horticultural Society, whose gardens formed such an important attraction, withdrew its support. Finally, the competition of the enormous Viennese exhibition in 1873 proved too much and by the following year the *Examiner* newspaper reported that 'the novelty has worn off'. The proposed 1875 exhibition was cancelled and the series closed in 1874 with an overall loss of £150,000 which had to be met by the Royal Commissioners.

The Polytechnic Exhibition of Moscow in 1872 also attempted to move away from the established tradition of one central exhibition hall by housing each category in a separate

building. The Society of Friends of Natural Science, Anthropology and Ethnography of the Imperial University of Moscow held the exhibition to celebrate the bicentennial of the birth of Peter the Great. They hoped that the exhibits could later be used to form the Central Polytechnic Museum and consequently excluded Fine Art. The categories chosen included Geologo-Mineralogical and Mining, Technological and Applied Physics, Botanical and Horticultural, and Arboricultural; and although these specific categories may not all have formed precedents for future exhibition organizers, the process of decentralization became increasingly popular.

The Vienna exhibition of 1873 was one of the first international events to follow the Russian example of locating exhibits separately. The organizers built Machinery, Fine Art and Agricultural halls, as well as the main Palace of Industry, and as at Paris in 1867, these were then surrounded by many smaller buildings and constructions erected by the participating countries. The number and variety of these additional attractions was greatly enhanced by the mature woodland of the Prater exhibition site and even more by the cosmopolitan flavour of Vienna. The list of exhibitors included countries from the Near, Middle and Far East and H.C. Sweny was able to sum it up in his appendix to the official British Report on the exhibition thus:

It may well be doubted whether the practical and the picturesque, the modern and the medieval, the East and the West will ever again mingle in one harmonious whole, with such equal aid from art and nature, as on the Prater of 1873, in the Buildings in the Park.

During the preceding decades Vienna had become a modern metropolis with many new buildings, including the splendid Opera House (where the family Strauss ruled supreme) and the future use of the main exhibition buildings had been decided before they were constructed. The huge conical wrought iron domed rotunda at the centre of the main Industry Palace was scheduled to be Vienna's future Corn Exchange, while the Machinery

37. Gas bracket by Ratcliff & Tyler of Birmingham, 'very admirable in design – the product of a true artist'. Vienna 1873. (*Art Journal*, 1873)

Hall was earmarked for use as a freight or grain store for the Great Northern Railway.

The River Danube itself was the scene of major improvements, including the re-alignment of its main channel half a mile nearer the city centre. The 500,000 cubic feet of gravel removed was used for the exhibition site on the Prater, or Imperial Park, next to the river.

The great Palace of Industry was designed by Charles Hasenaur in the Italian Renaissance style, with highly finished plaster decorations on its outside faces. Inside, the main 2,953 foot long nave ran in an east–west direction, with its galleries in the form of sixteen transepts. The exhibits were displayed according to a simple system. Each country was put in direct geographical position to its neighbours, so that a basic knowledge of the world sufficed to find the location of any country's exhibit.

The Palace's rotunda, which had been designed by John Scott Russell, Secretary to the 1851 Commissioners, had obviously been inspired by the 'official' 1851 building plan which it strongly resembled. The immense conical dome over the rotunda, constructed of wrought iron, was 354 feet in diameter, the largest ever built. On top of this was a central lantern 101 feet in diameter with a smaller 25 foot diameter lantern on top of that, the whole being surmounted by a gigantic copy of the Austrian crown, made from wrought iron plate, gilded and decorated with glass imitations of the crown jewels. The underside of the roof was covered with canvas painted to represent frescoes – the same basic technique as that used at the 1853–54 New York Exhibition – while the floor of the rotunda was lower than the exhibition galleries and had a highly ornamental fountain in the centre. The number of exhibits inside the rotunda did not justify the immense costs of building such a large and elaborate structure, and three years later the Plans and Architecture Committee of the Philadelphia Exhibition referred to it indirectly as a wasteful architectural memorial. But the design of other exhibition buildings was generally dull and uninspired, and as it had been necessary to cover over some of the beautiful garden courts between the transepts to increase exhibiting space, the general extravagance of the rotunda undoubtedly added some much-needed colour and interest.

At the 1867 Paris Exposition Universelle one of the most popular exhibits had been the large scale model of the Suez Canal, complete with ships passing through it. Not to be outdone, the Italians brought to Vienna an enormous model of their latest engineering masterpiece, the entrance to the Mont Cenis Tunnel including all the railway lines, signals, and equipment and even a train. But in general it was the range of goods displayed rather than particular items which attracted the crowds.

Nobody could have been so interested in the exhibits as the Japanese. On their return to Japan the sixty-six technical engineers in the official delegation produced a monumental 96-volume report on the exhibition, effectively providing Japan with the necessary information to set her on the way to becoming a fully industrialised nation.

Potentially one of the most spectacular exhibitions held to this date, the Vienna International Exhibition suffered from a number of external disasters. The first was the effect of the dramatic collapse of the Vienna Stock Exchange only nine days after the Austrian Emperor, Franz Joseph I, had opened the exhibition. The end of the Civil War in America had resulted in a great spurt of economic growth in North America using mostly European capital and English supplies, particularly in the construction of railways. A lot of the financing had been carried out on paper credit and when the Bank of England first became aware of the warning signs it stopped the flow of capital, which in turn caused the New York Stock Exchange to cease trading on 20 September 1872 following the failure of a number of American banks. Two months later the slump hit London and six months later Vienna suffered a total collapse of her Bourse following wild speculation after the closure of many of the Austrian banks. In addition, many foreigners fearing a re-occurrence of the 1872 cholera outbreak, decided not to visit Vienna. The third, and possibly decisive, reason for discontent was the attitude of the Viennese hoteliers and restaurateurs who raised their prices to such heights that even wealthy tourists were effectively driven off. The final accounts of the exhibition showed an income of only one sixth of the actual cost of the event, making it one of the great financial failures of the nineteenth century.

On 9 May 1865 the second Dublin International Exhibition was opened by the Prince of Wales, later King Edward VII. It was financed by a member of the famous brewery family, Sir Benjamin Lee Guinness, who had only just finished paying for the refurbishing of Dublin's St Patrick's Cathedral.

Two buildings in Coburg Gardens housed the exhibition. The main structure was made of brick and stone. To the rear of it was a winter garden and exhibition building in iron and glass which the organizers, The Winter Garden Company (a private company) had intended to use as the home of a permanent exhibition in Dublin. However, eighteen years later it was dismantled and re-erected opposite Battersea Park, London where it opened in 1885 as the Albert Palace of Science and Art, only to be demolished nine years later.

There was also an exhibition in Dunedin, New Zealand, in 1865 following the 1861–63 gold rush. This was one of the many small exhibitions then being organized in the Southern Hemisphere which were to culminate in much larger international exhibitions in Australia.

The next significant international exhibition was held in Philadelphia in 1876 to celebrate the centenary of the U.S.A. The suggestion was first made by Professor J. L. Campbell in 1866, but no further steps were taken until 11 August 1869 when the Board of Management of Philadelphia's Franklin Institute discussed the proposals and pledged itself to the project. It formed a special organizing committee, issued a letter setting out its proposals to the Select and Common Councils of the City of Philadelphia (even requesting that space in Philadelphia's Fairmount Park be made available), and asked that official representation should be made to Congress in Washington on the matter.

As a result a joint commission was set up with representatives from the City of Philadelphia, the State Legislature at Harrisburg, and the Franklin Institute. The Commission presented its case to a select committee of the American Congress in Washington, and on 3 March 1871, an Act of Congress was passed 'to provide for celebrating the one hundredth anniversary of the American Independence, by holding an International Exhibition of Arts, Manufactures, and Products of the Soil and Mine, in the City of Philadelphia, and State of Pennsylvania, in the year eighteen hundred and seventy-six'. The Act also set up a panel of Commissioners who finally met for eight days at the Continental Hotel in Philadelphia in March 1872 and worked out a plan of operation, including the setting up and instructing of a Committee on Plans and Architecture to produce a design for a building based on the Paris 1867 classification system and covering about 50 acres.

38. Alexander Graham Bell's centennial telephone. (Replica from Science Museum, London) Philadelphia 1876. (Crown copyright)

A second meeting was held at the end of May 1872 because lack of funds was holding back any real progress (the Plans and Architecture Committee had been unable to proceed at all). The Commissioners again applied to Congress for the setting up of a Centennial Board of Finance which would allow them to raise funds 'for the preparation and conduct of the Exposition' and which empowered them to secure subscriptions of capital stock up to $10,000,000 which was to be made available to the general public in $10 shares: thus financing the entire venture by direct contribution from the American people.

In 1873 visits were made to the Vienna Exhibition by Professor W. P. Blake, a member of the Commission who had been involved with the 1867 Paris exhibition, Henry Pettit, the Commission's consultant civil engineer, who was specially instructed to study the planning and construction techniques used at Vienna, and Herman Joseph Schwarzmann, Engineer of Design to the Fairmount Park Commissioners. Schwarzmann had planned much of the park, including its zoo – the first to be built in America – and although he was only twenty-seven he was made responsible for the planning and layout of the exhibition grounds, as well as the design of the Arts Building (Memorial Hall), the Horticultural Building and other smaller structures. In fact he created in Philadelphia the first properly landscaped and planned international exhibition. The organization of the whole exhibition reflected his careful attention to detail. Proper regard was taken of such mundane requirements as the provision of adequate accommodation, transportation and facilities for visitors, both on and off the site. Even the medal system was rationalized so that only one type of medal was awarded accompanied by a certificate setting out the exact reasons for its award.

The question of the designs for the other exhibition buildings, however, had produced considerable confusion. An unlimited public competition was held for designs for the main

39. Ground plan of the Centennial Exposition. Philadelphia 1876. (*The Masterpieces of the Exhibition*, 1876)

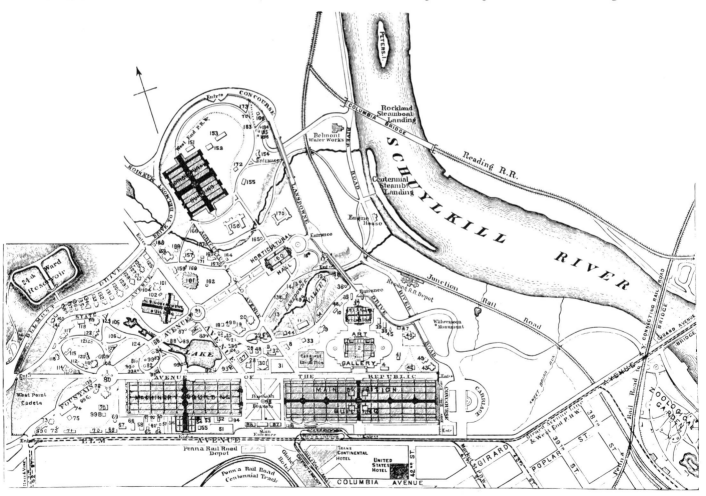

building and forty-three plans were submitted. Of these, ten received $1,000 prize money and were admitted to a second competition, which was won by the team of Collins & Autenreith. However they were given no specific instructions to develop their scheme. Instead the Committee members changed their minds and adopted Schwarzmann's overall plan of individual pavilions in the style of the Moscow Polytechnic Exhibition of 1872. For the main building they took a design submitted by Vaux & Radford of New York for the first competition, added an idea put forward by the fourth overall prizewinners Messrs H. A. & J. P. Sims, and sent the resulting hybrid to the Commissioners for approval in November 1873. They also issued a general instruction that 'domes, towers and central massive features' were to be 'ignored as too ambitious and expensive, and the building to trust for its impressiveness to its great size and proper treatment of its elevations, and to its interior vistas and arrangements, and not to have any central feature erected at great expense for only a few months' – the Vienna trips had certainly driven one lesson home!

The confusions were by no means over. Messrs Vaux & Radford produced three schemes for the main building based on their suggested design, but with varying construction techniques. Without referring to them, the Committee then asked Henry Pettit to produce a fourth scheme based on the simplest of the three, but including some alterations he had previously proposed. Eventually the Committee decided to go ahead with Pettit's scheme although it was slightly more expensive than Vaux & Radford's simplest design. Vaux & Radford then resigned and Pettit and his partner Joseph Wilson, both engineers, found themselves designers of the main building having not even entered a scheme in the original competition! They were also to be responsible for the design of the Machinery Hall, the bridges over the Lansdowne and Belmont Ravines in Fairmount Park, and some of the planning and layout work as well. As the entire layout and all the main buildings were now being designed by either a landscape architect or engineers, there was tremendous uproar in architectural circles! All the argument and the lack of money had wasted a great deal of time, but with the decisions finally made, work went ahead immediately. Bureaucratic red tape was simply ignored, and problems were left to resolve themselves afterwards. Both the Memorial Hall and the Main Exhibition Building were found to be too small. An extension was added to the Memorial Hall while the Main Building was increased in area, the central portion raised and towers added to break the monotony, effectively defeating the instructions of the Plans and Architecture Committee. Three other main buildings, housing the Art, Horticultural and Agricultural exhibits were also designed and by June 1875 the five main structures were well under way, all due for completion by 1 January 1876. The 236 acres of Fairmount Park that were set aside for the main exhibition area were surrounded by fencing and before long construction began on the other 250 smaller pavilions and buildings. It is amazing to note that they were all completed in about nine months. Almost the only section of the exhibition that was not finished was the landscape gardening.

The pavilions of the foreign participants and the American States were the first which modern eyes would consider suitable for an international exhibition. It is particularly interesting to note the absence at Philadelphia of Colonial revival buildings among the States' pavilions – the first and last time that any State was to produce a building designed on modern lines at an American international exhibition. The American Government erected a large pavilion to hold the exhibits of various government departments, amongst them the original document of the Declaration of Independence, exhibits on the American Indians, displays of fresh fruit, fish and vegetables on view through the glass sides of gigantic refrigerators, and archaeological displays of the newly-discovered dwellers of the cave-cities of Mesa Verde. Elsewhere on the site were the ingredients that have come to be associated with American Fairs and enjoyment: cigars and popcorn were on sale from specially built kiosks, and soda-water was available from the white or coloured marble stands with silver mountings, which were scattered throughout the main building, but as in 1851, alcoholic beverages were not available.

The Women's Centennial Executive Committee, led by the energetic Mrs Gillespie, not only organized the Women's Pavilion but was also responsible for the collection of a great deal of money for the enterprise, and the selling of many hundreds of exhibition shares. They also commissioned the Centennial Inauguration March from Richard Wagner which was played at the opening ceremony on 10 May 1876. Joseph Wilson, Henry Pettit's partner, felt that 'to one who is an enthusiastic admirer of Wagner, it must be confessed that it is somewhat disappointing. Still, it *is* Wagner. None can dispute that. The grand clashes, swelling up and up until they almost overtop the heavens themselves'.

The strict adherence of the Women's Committee to their policy of using only female labour in their pavilion caused problems when it came to finding someone to look after the

40. President Grant and the Emperor of Brazil starting the great Corlis Engine in Machinery Hall. Philadelphia 1876. (Frank Leslie's *Illustrated Historical Register of the Centennial Exposition*, 1876)

41. The colossal hand and torch of the Statue of Liberty exhibited to help raise funds for the statue's completion. Philadelphia 1876. (Stereo photograph by the Centennial Photographic Co., 1876)

six horsepower steam engine that drove the looms and spinning frames. They finally found Miss Emma Allison of Grimsby, Ontario, a girl 'highly educated . . . in theoretical as well as practical engineering (who) offered an example . . . to the engineers of the male sex in the neatness of her dress and . . . the cleanliness exhibited in both engine and engineroom'. (6)

After the usual preliminaries of the playing of the national anthems of all the participating countries, the blessing of the exhibition and the singing of the centennial hymn, the exhibition was opened by President Grant, accompanied by Dom Pedro, the Brazilian Emperor. The two leaders then went on a conducted tour of the exhibition. Their main objective was the Corlis Engine in the Machinery Hall. There, at a given signal from Mr George Corlis, the designer of the gigantic engine, first the Emperor and then the President turned on the steam and the giant pistons gradually started turning the many wheels and bands connecting the engine to the machinery displayed in the hall, and bringing the whole display to life.

The exhibition had many new inventions to show its visitors, including heavy machinery, agricultural equipment, the first sewing machine (there was even a statue of its inventor, Elias Howe, in the grounds), the first practical typewriter, and Alexander Graham Bell's Telephone – although few took any notice of it, preferring to remark on a more conventional box of conjuring tricks displayed nearby. Elsewhere in the Machinery Hall, with its impressive Cataract pumping equipment sending streams of water down into the specially built ten foot deep tank, the display reflected the outstanding advances made in the last few years and, particularly noticeable to us looking back at it all today, the beginnings of the ingenuity and invention of the Americans which was to make them the mass-production centre of the world a few decades later.

The exhibition in the permanent Memorial Hall Art Pavilion resulted in a complete re-awakening of artistic appreciation in a country that until then had had little time for such things. Art Schools and local art societies sprang up all over America, young men from many parts of America went to study in Europe, particularly in Paris, and American artists of the stature of Copely and West were finally recognized in their native land. But for many people the artistic triumph was the high-relief bust of a beautiful girl made from butter by a Mrs Brooks of Arkansas! She visited the exhibition towards the end of its run and turned yet another 'shapeless, golden mass' of butter into another sleeping beauty, using only 'paddles, cedar sticks, broom straws and camels' hair', and all in the space of an hour and a quarter!

Bartholdi, the French sculptor, had designed a great green cast-iron fountain for the centre of the plaza between the Main Building and Machinery Hall, and also had the torch

42. The Elevated Railway across the Lansdowne Ravine. Philadelphia 1876. (*The Masterpieces of the Exhibition*, 1876)

56

arm of his Statue of Liberty on show. For a small charge one could get a preview of standing in the gallery at the base of the torch. This proved one of the star attractions of the exposition.

Fairmount Park, which even allowing for the 236 acres of the exhibition was only partly filled, provided a fully mature setting which could be viewed to great effect from the specially erected elevator on Belmont Hill. This carried forty people 185 feet up to the top of the observation building for a bird's-eye view.

The exhibition even boasted its own narrow gauge internal railway system and, even more prophetic of future international exhibition monorail transport, an elevated railway invented by General Roy Stone of Elmira, New York State. It carried sixty people riding on a specially designed and manufactured car and engine running on three rails on a triangular section bridge over the Belmont Ravine between the Agricultural and Horticultural Halls. It took two minutes to complete the 500 foot crossing over the 30 foot ravine and cost 3 cents each way.

Some people had been worried that the reason for the celebrations would stop countries from exhibiting, but rather it was the high import tariffs which kept people away. The exhibition managed to cover its own costs from grants from Federal, State and City funds, the money taken at the gates, and the sale of various concessions, such as official photography and official souvenirs, which were to become so important in the financing of many future fairs and exhibitions.

All in all it was a splendid birthday party although one of the Japanese visitors obviously found the crowds a bit excessive, writing home that 'The crowds, some like sheep, run here, run there. One man start, one thousand follow. Nobody can see anything, nobody can do anything. All rush, push, tear, shout, make plenty noise, say ''damn great'' many times, get very tired and go home'.

Today there is little left to remind Americans of their Centennial Exposition. The Main Building was torn down in 1880, and the Moorish-style Horticultural Building, with its barley-sugar stick twisted columns, coloured bricks, ferns and statuary, lasted until its wanton destruction in 1955. Today the only reminders left in Fairmount Park, apart from a few statues and fountains, are the Ohio State Building and the Fine Art Pavilion, now renamed Memorial Hall. Hidden in its basement is a splendid model of the whole Exposition made after it closed by students of a local architectural college.

Some of the exhibits can still be seen in Washington. Seventy-eight wagons filled with exhibits were sent to the Smithsonian Institute at the close of the exhibition. But most of these were either agricultural or mineral exhibits and apart from the splendid ethnic display from Peru which included a number of shrunken human heads (which subsequently caused the Smithsonian some embarrassment), there is little that the Institute was able to bring straight from its stores for the large bicentennial reconstruction of a typical section of the Centennial Exposition.

43. 'The Chap who attempts to do the Exhibition in one day'. Philadelphia 1876. (*Going to the Centennial*, Small, 1876)

CHAPTER FIVE
Paris, Australia and all the World

'There will be time enough', I said, 'for guides and catalogues by and by. For the nonce let us go and see all the fun of the fair.'

George Augustus Sala, 1878

After the Franco–Prussian war and the savage destruction of the Commune, both of which left France badly shaken, the new Government of the Third Republic felt it was necessary to show the world that France was still an important cultural and political centre. To this end it mounted the 1878 Paris Exposition Universelle. France could neither afford the cost nor the effort while she was still rebuilding and recovering from the humiliating effects of war, and the final loss of nearly 32 million francs must have seemed ample justification for its detractors. However the Government, which bore the expense, felt that the exhibition had achieved its purpose. Certainly Mr George Hadfield of Ross-on-Wye brought away the desired impression 'Everything on this visit struck me amazingly. The French are certainly a great people. The Exhibition must affect everyone with the greatest wonder.'

44. Bird's-eye view of Paris and the 1878 Exposition. (*The Graphic*, 1878)

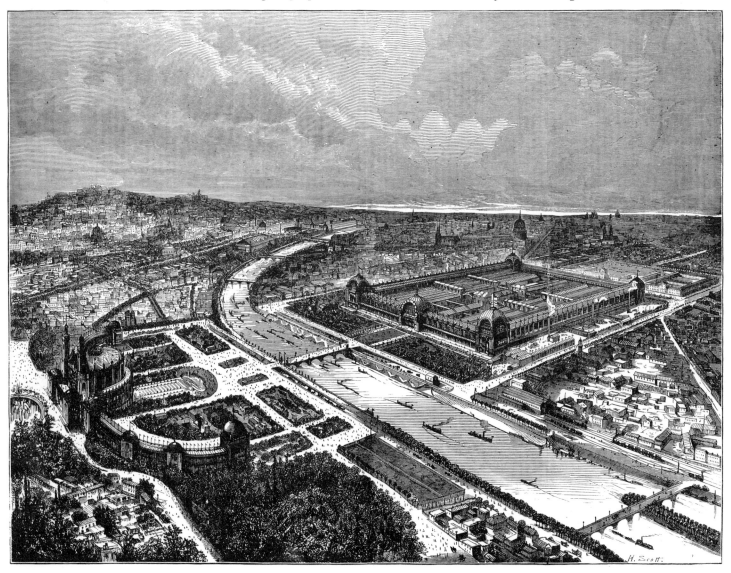

.There were many remarkable features, such as gigantic cascade down the south-east face of the Trocadero Hill which sent more than 61,000 gallons of water crashing down each hour to the river below. But it was the main exhibition building itself that formed the most spectacular structure. Whilst allowing a number of kiosks and other small buildings around the main palace and on the Trocadéro Hill, the organizers under M.J.B.Krantz, the Commissaire-Général who had been the chief designer of the 1867 building, abandoned the new idea of decentralization and returned to the traditional method of housing the exhibition in one building. They did, however, incorporate some of the popular features of the 1867 individual national buildings into the main palace. Here, overlooking the central courtyard, they allowed each nation to erect a façade to its display, resulting in a grand 'Rue des Nations' which had 'all the beauty and interest of the individual countries' architectural styles grouped into one gigantic street front.

As in 1851 an architectural competition was held for the design of the main building and, as in 1851, the main building incorporated some of the ideas of the ninety-four entrants, but was designed by none of them. The plan of the building reflected Prince Napoleon's theoretical layout – his original grid plan was used, although the 1878 building was of rectangular design. At long last the engineers had found a way of taking the roofing stresses of their building down through the foundations without relying on either large leads weights or on complicated tie-beam systems. The French engineer De Dion, who unfortunately died just before the opening of the exhibition, had developed a method of creating the necessary strength in framework girders and in many ways the whole structure

45. General view of the Rue des Nations in the central courtyard of the main building. Paris 1878. (*L'Exposition Universelle de 1878 Illustrée*)

59

46. A clock and candelabra set in bronze by the Paris firm of Baques. Paris 1878. (*Art Journal*, 1878)

of the building resembled the inverted hull of a modern steel ship. Eiffel was once again involved in the details of the building, and it was he who designed the curved sheet-metal roof of the main entrance and the side pavilions – a feature which was unpopular at the time – and the short north-east and south-west side vestibules. The remainder of the building and the overall design were under the control of the French architect M. Hardy. He was responsible for two innovations which were hidden from the public eye. The first was a complete network of rails inside the building to assist in the transport and placement of the exhibits. The rails were covered over during the exhibition's run and then uncovered after it closed, much to the surprise of the editor of the *Art Journal*, 'Nor can I easily forget the strange effect when, on returning to the Champ de Mars a week after its formal closing, I heard the whistle of an engine in one of the most beautiful and retired corners of the gardens, and beheld labourers tearing up the smooth walks and disclosing the rails beneath; whilst inside the building the flooring had almost disappeared, and cases were being rolled on handcarts along the rails that had then suddenly come to view.'

The second innovation provided the solution to building problems and permitted the construction of a new, and beneficial, ventilation system. Not only did the Champ de Mars slope down to the Seine, but as a result of the 1867 exhibition and the turmoil of the 1870–71 troubles, it was a mass of holes. Undeterred M. Hardy placed the ground floor of his exhibition building about ten feet above the roughly-levelled ground and used the space below for twenty giant pipes, each 12ft 6in. in diameter, which ventilated the entire exhibition using four huge fans. He thus overcame the original problem, managed to keep the temperature at a comfortable level (always 8° Centigrade lower than outside, even on the hottest days), was able to provide water through other pipes below the floor, and at the same time gave the entire exhibition a more imposing frontage by placing it on a raised terrace.

Decorative columns embellished the façades of the building, helping to relieve the enormous expanses of glass wall and hide the structural supports. Each symbolically represented one of the participating nations 'contributing a column to the common edifice. The idea was carried out by a colossal statue at the base characteristic of a country, surmounted by its shield, and its banner floating above. The conception was fine, the types in the main well rendered, and the statues stood as though guarding the twenty entrances which on each side of the large central one led from the terrace into the building.'(1)

More than any previous exhibition, Paris 1878 was almost totally dominated by large manufacturers and great businesses all eager to sell their wares, and there were far fewer individual exhibitors. As George Augustus Sala remarked at the time in one of his articles for the *Daily Telegraph* 'You look in vain in these interminable corridors of shop-windows

47. 'Orchestraphone' by James Hiller of Camden Town, London, 'a reed organ with two manuals, containing twenty-five stops with thirteen sets of reeds (of two and a half octaves), two knee swells and two heel-movement pedals'. Paris 1878. (*Art Journal*, 1878)

for such naive specimens of individual ingenuity and labour as were delightfully manifest in our World's Fair in Hyde Park seven-and-twenty years ago – models of Tintern Abbey or Rochester Castle in cork; Pharoah and all his Host engulfed in the Red Sea, burnt with a red-hot poker on a deal board by a clergyman in the vale of Taunton; Comical Creatures from Wurtemberg; Gulliver and the Lilliputians in wax; Susanna and the Elders in Berlin wool, by a Lady Twenty-five years Bedridden; or a Model in Ivory of the Old Temeraire, by Two Congenital Idiots. These were unpretending "Exhibits" enough; but they spoke of the craft and patience of individual Man. In more recent Expositions, and notable in the gigantic Bazaar which I am at present painfully exploring, individual man, save in a very few instances, disappears, and is replaced by great Companies and great Firms solicitous of orders.' (2)

The sheer quantity and range of goods exhibited was becoming unwieldy, and even Prince Napoleon's system of classification failed to help the dazed visitor find his way amongst the miles of glass cases and displays. The sheer worry of getting lost must have added to the exhaustion of the average visitor, 'S was very tired and quite knocked up . . . very tired with constant walking . . .' (3) Almost the only means of seeing the exhibition without walking was to hire one of the 'fauteuils roulants' powered by a friendly trundler. Even the national restaurants were unable to offer inexpensive resting places. They had

48. Linoleum designs by Messrs Treloar. Paris 1878. (*Art Journal*, 1878)

62

49 & 50. Original sketch and finished stand for William Watt of London, designed by E. W. Godwin and painted by James Abbot McNeill Whistler in *Harmony in Yellow and Gold*. Paris 1878. (Victoria and Albert Museum, London)

become commercialized and did not offer anything like the value and authenticity of 1867. Sala had so much trouble that he even went as far as deploring the difference between the 'Republican commissariat of M. Krantz in '78 and the Imperialist commissariat of M. le Play in '67! Ah, days when we used to christen the exterior zone of the old exhibition "Grub-Street"! ... Paris is regenerated; and one of the greatest difficulties to be encountered in Paris just now, both in and out of the Exhibition, is to get a decent dinner.' (4) About the only easily available, free restorative was provided by the Pavilion of Mineral Waters where six different types of French natural mineral waters were available. Alternatively the visitor could gaze hopefully at the Japanese fountain with its wooden ladles, and water pouring forth from a model flower blossom on a section of tree trunk into a giant conch shell.

Since there was no main route around the exhibits some of the unusual exhibits became important landmarks for the visitors – central points to which they returned again and again before setting out once more round another section. Two such landmarks were pieces

51. Gustave Doré's vase, 'brimming with the false felicities of love and wine'. Paris 1878 (*Art Journal*, 1878)

of sculptural art. One was a colossal vase designed by Gustave Doré and covered with 'flower-branches, by the aid of which mortals of both sexes, unencumbered with vestments, toil in spasmodic effort to ascend, while Cupids circle about to encourage or thwart,' (5) – a truly Bacchanalian concept! The other was a direct copy of the State of Victoria's gold obelisk exhibited at London's 1862 Exhibition. This time it represented the amount of gold used by a Parisian jeweller each year in his business – an obvious example of the influx of trade and commerce. The evolutionary change away from the high principled, educational displays, eccentricities, and individualistic atmospheres, had begun, although the lack of amusement at Paris in 1878 might not have directly indicated it to the casual observer.

The theme of the exhibition was certainly high principled – the peace so desired in Europe. Although there was no official German exhibit because of the recent Franco–Prussian troubles, some German painters, in the spirit of the exhibition, did send their work to the Fine Art department. The organizers commissioned a hymn of praise to Peace for the opening ceremony, and used her image to decorate the frieze around the specially-built Trocadéro Palace. This was a gigantic air-conditioned conference and concert centre illuminated by 4,000 gas lamps (one for each member of a full capacity audience). One of the many conferences held was the Congrès Internationale pour l'Amélioreation du sort des Aveugles which resulted in international adoption of the use of the Braille system of touch-reading.

The towers of the Trocadéro Palace provided the public with ever popular bird's-eye views of the exhibition. The unusual circular hydraulic lifts were worked by the same pumps as the cascade, using water from the Seine. Amongst the small exterior kiosks and displays, the public could also see the head of Bartholdi's 'Statue of Liberty enlightening the World', newly finished and awaiting transport to New York and a splendid clock from Norway with a filigree wood case and a supporting tower clad in cedar shingles.

The exhibition was partly financed by the proceeds of a special lottery. Most of the prizes were purchased from or donated by the exhibitors, and included diamond necklaces and a ton of carbonate of soda. The terrific range and number of odd prizes gave the cartoonists a field day since the non-prizewinners seemed almost in the minority!

Although there was not the general joie-de-vivre of the Paris of 1867, perhaps Frédéric le Play was more satisfied. In 1867, he had felt that the amusements, sideshows and general bawdiness of some of the exhibits, which had merely mirrored the Paris of the time, were quite out of keeping with his idea of the aims of the event – lofty heights of co-existence, peace and human development. One wonders how he would have viewed some of the public relations-orientated shows of today which are the result of the ever growing involvement of big business in international expositions since 1867.

On the other side of the world a far more basic form of commerce was responsible for the first antipodean international exhibition. In the early months of 1851 Edmund Hammond Hargreaves had first found alluvial gold on a tributary of the Macquarie River near Bathurst in New South Wales. He was one of the many prospectors who had made the dash West in the 1848 American gold rush, and soon realized that the similarity of terrain between the California goldfields and his native New South Wales could quite possibly lead to riches nearer home. Other prospectors laughed at his naïvety but within a week of landing back at Sydney, he had proved his point.

The effect was dramatic; immigration trebled the population within a decade; British exports to Australia multiplied five fold in two years; and the colony, which until then had been primarily a convict settlement, was on the map. By the mid-1860s Australia was supplying a sixth of Britain's wool as well as a third of the world's gold. It was against this background that Sydney, her major city, became the site of the first of a series of Australian International Exhibitions. The Agricultural Society of New South Wales had first started holding annual shows in 1870 and by 1877 had exhibits from New Zealand, Fiji, Ceylon and Canada. It was as a direct result of the success of this exhibition that a proposal for an international exhibition in Sydney in 1879 was put forward.

Just as there was much public argument about the siting of the Sydney Opera House,

Plate I
The Great French Conservatory. A contemporary coloured chromolithograph by Boguard. Paris 1867.

Plate II
The International Exhibition, Dublin 1865. (*Illustrated London News*, 1865)

Grande Serre Française

53. The Exposition Lottery. A Lucky Prize-winner: 'Sir, you have gained a prize entitling you to have twelve teeth drawn without any charge' cartoon by Cham. Paris 1878. (*Paris Herself Again*, Sala, G. A., 1880)

there was a public outcry in 1879 about the building of the exhibition's Garden Palace in what was then the Outer Domain of Government House, and is today part of the Royal Botanic Gardens. This Palace, designed by James Barnet, was a huge structure for the time and many feared it would completely ruin the aspect of Sydney's beautiful natural harbour. The 100 foot diameter dome was supported on the perimeter by four smaller viewing towers decorated with flags and streamers, with two smaller minarets similarly decorated on each side. The dome and the main tower were constructed in permanent masonry, but the remainder of the building was made in wood. The Palace was cruciform in plan and in addition to the ground level space there were first floor galleries along the sides, while the slope of the site was used to provide a basement under the eastern half of the building. On the basement level, under the central dome, was a fountain surmounted by a statue of Queen Victoria. It could be looked down on through an opening in the main floor and formed the central axis and landmark of the exhibition.

When one remembers that the distance from Europe to Australia involved a journey of up to three months, and that the population of Australia, even after the gold rush, was still only a little over 2,250,000, it is surprising that there were any foreign exhibits at all. Yet so strong was the lure of gold that the number of British exhibitors in the industrial section was greater than the number at the American Centennial Exposition in 1876! (But the distances and consequent high cost of communication with Head Office were great enough to cause them to appeal, unsuccessfully, to the British Parliament for a special 50% exhibition rate for their cables from Sydney to London!)

The Commissioners of both Victoria and New South Wales had taken the chance offered them in Paris in 1878 to invite as many foreign nations as possible to participate in the Sydney exhibition as well as in the Melbourne one a year later. They must have been well satisfied with the response since all the great European nations, the United States of America, Japan, India and the other British colonies, as well as the Australian colonies and New Zealand, were all represented.

Among the exhibits were the usual items of everyday Victorian life and work but made with special reference to Australian conditions. High class furnishings and clever inventions were shown alongside more mundane and earthy exhibits, like 'Spratt's patent food for fowls', tools for mines, sporting guns and rifles, and even improved sleeping berths for emigrant ships. Perhaps one of the more unusual exhibits in the circumstances was the three year old Devon bull sent by Mr Yeo of Barnstaple, which won first prize in the stock class. One can only wonder at the care and expertise that allowed him to survive the journey let alone win the championship!

On pages 66 and 67
52. The Australian International Exhibition building at Sydney. (*The Graphic*, 1879)

54. The Melbourne International Exhibition, 1880. (*The Graphic* 1880)

Opened on 17 September 1879 for six months, the exhibition building spent the next two years as an auditorium and as home of Australia's first Mining and Technological Museum and the basement as government offices and stores. Then on 22 September 1882 it was burnt to the ground. A clue to the cause of the fire was thought by many people to be the convict files stored there. When the ruins were removed the site became part of the Royal Botanic Gardens with the name Palace Garden in memory of the great edifice.

In August 1851, only a few months after Hargreaves had found it in New South Wales, gold was also discovered at Ballarat, sixty miles from Melbourne, and over the next fifteen years Victoria became the gold supplier to a large section of the world and the best known colony in the British Empire. A series of local and subsequently national exhibitions had been held in Melbourne at irregular intervals since 1850, but in 1855, on the crest of the gold discoveries, a larger show took place on the site of the present Royal Mint in William Street. It was open for thirty days and 40,000 people visited it to view the industrial and indigenous products of the colony. A similar event in 1861, open for twice the time and seen by over 67,000 people, led to a series of Inter-Colonial Exhibitions which were held in a new, larger building in 1866, 1872 and 1875. Then in 1877 a plan was submitted to the Colonial Parliament for the erection of a new, permanent building to be opened with a grand International Exhibition in 1879.

A large and influential commission was set up and on 19 February 1879 the foundation stone was laid in the presence of 10,000 people. Designed by the architects Reed & Barnes on a plan similar to that of Sydney's, the building and its annexes provided a floor space of about 22 acres. The edifice still stands on the original site in Carlton Gardens facing on to Victoria Parade, providing the city of Melbourne with its main exhibition and conference venue. It has seen many celebrations over the past ninety-six years, including the opening of the first Australian Federal Parliament.

The holding of such an exhibition in a city which had existed for less than fifty years was a striking achievement, and the Marquis of Normanby, the Governor of Victoria, acknowledged this in his opening address on 1 October 1880: 'It must be a source of legitimate pride to the people of Victoria that a Colony whose territory was an unknown land less than half a century ago has been enabled by the wealth of its natural resources, the wisdom of its laws, and the enterprise, intelligence and industry of its population, to bring to a successful completion this grand project.' (6)

George Collins Levey, the Secretary of the Exhibition Commission, had secured international publicity for the event by spending a year travelling through North America and Europe, persuading nations and individuals to participate. His efforts, and those of the organizing Commissioners, were well rewarded. 'When the opening cantata was sung, and the doors thrown open, the long vista of the Avenue of Nations revealed a scene of exhilarating magnificence. Great Britain, France, Germany, Austria, Belgium, Holland, Italy, Switzerland, Denmark, Russia, Norway, Portugal, Spain, Sweden, Turkey, all contributed to the mass of the gay effect – some of them at lavish expense and with delightful good taste. The United States made a brilliant display, and so did India; and other colonies lent their aid – New South Wales, Queensland, South Australia, Tasmania, Western Australia, New Zealand, Fiji, Cape Colony, the Straits Settlements, Ceylon, Mauritius, and the South Sea Islands; and the Japanese indicated their friendly feeling and their extraordinary skill in a charming court of their own.' (7) Careful landscaping around the main building with wide avenues, flowerbeds, ponds and fountains, and the kiosks with fluttering pennants gave the whole exhibition a colourful, carnival atmosphere.

The art exhibits which had been sent from Britain for the Sydney exhibitions were also shown at Melbourne, having spent part of the intervening time on show at the Queensland exhibition in Brisbane in July 1880. They subsequently went on to be shown in the new public library building in Adelaide, South Australia. Some £14,000 worth of these pictures were actually sold at the exhibitions, many of them to public art galleries, and other pictures, like the twenty-nine James Barry etchings sent by the London Society of Arts and given to the Melbourne National Gallery, were presented to various Australian art galleries.

Unlike the Sydney exhibition which was very agriculturally orientated, the Melbourne exhibition was more concerned with industry and the manufacturers of Victoria, who even then were earning £13,000,000 per annum for their products, found that in comparison with many foreign products they could already hold their own. The exhibition also gave them an unequalled opportunity to find the answers to their weaknesses: a contemporary chronicler noted that it was 'a most interesting feature to observe the intelligent workman spending his holiday in a careful and elaborate investigation of the specialities and novelties of design, of material, and of process which gave to goods of foreign manufacture some peculiar excellence of whose existence he had perhaps not formerly been aware.' (8)

The number of visitors, who were counted on a newly patented registering machine as they entered the turnstiles, was nearly four times as large, in terms of percentage of population, as at the Paris exhibition of 1878 and about six times as great as at any of the preceding ones. The effects of the exhibitions were considerable, both on the Australians and on the foreigners. Of particular importance was the opening up of direct trade with Germany, America, France and Belgium, and the start of regular steamship services between Australia and Marseilles and Bremen. Some French banks even opened branches in Melbourne and Sydney. Trade before this had always been through the merchants and traders of the mother country – now the colonies were adopting a more independent position.

M. Jules Joubert, an artistic and volatile adventurer and entrepreneur who had made and lost two or three fortunes, had been Secretary of the Agricultural Society of New South Wales since 1867. It was he who first put forward the proposal for united Australian colonial representation at the Philadelphia exhibition in 1876, and in 1878 he had been Secretary to the New South Wales Commissioners to the Paris Exhibition. There, with the other members of the Commission, he had been authorized on behalf of the Sydney Exhibition, to 'take such other steps as might be considered necessary to bring the exhibition under the notice of the various countries and collect exhibits.' The Sydney International Exhibition had been conceived and largely organized by Joubert thus far, and when he returned from Paris he was naturally disappointed to find that he had been excluded from the ranks of the 1879 Exhibition Commissioners, and stood charged with 'shipping out private property as returned exhibits'. After much argument he was also sacked by the Agricultural Society and finally left Sydney in disgust for Adelaide, where, with the help of Mr R. E. N. Twopenny, he organized South Australia's first international exhibition in 1881. Internationally it was an exceedingly small event but it did provide Joubert, Twopenny and their friends and relations with something to consider as a future source of power and wealth. At the end of 1881 they opened another exhibition in Perth, Western Australia, and then moved to New Zealand where the New Zealand International Exhibition of 1882 opened its doors at Christchurch under the 'private management of Messrs Joubert & Twopenny'. As the official record put it: 'From King Ahasuerus to Messrs Joubert & Twopenny, from 521 BC to the present year of grace – the history of exhibitions lies in this compass.'

For the rest of 1882–83 Joubert was busy organizing the Calcutta International Exhibition of 1883–84 before returning to Melbourne, building the Alexandra Theatre and going bankrupt once more in 1887. But in 1888 he was back in New South Wales to organize that colony's exhibits for the Melbourne Centennial International Exhibition.

He spent the following two years working in Dunedin and publishing his very aptly titled reminiscences *Shavings and Scrapes in Many Parts*, before moving on to Tasmania where he and his family organized two shows: one in Launceston in 1891–92 and a second in Hobart in 1894–95. His final effort, the Queensland International Exhibition, was held in Bowen Park, Brisbane, in 1897. He then settled in Melbourne where he died in 1907, having being involved in over fifty exhibitions during his lifetime. A few other people, like the American, C. B. Norton and Britain's Sir Philip Cunliffe Owen have participated in

55. Front cover of souvenir view book. Edinburgh 1886. (Banks & Co., 1886)

Opposite
Plate V
Title page from *L'Exposition de Paris (1900)*

Plate III
Chromolithograph of the 1889 Paris Exposition
Universelle. (Toronto Public Library Collection)

Plate IV
The Château d'Eau with the Palais de
l'Electricité behind it during one of the evening
displays. Paris 1900.

the organization and running of nearly as many exhibitions but for experience and excitement, to say nothing of nepotism, Jules Joubert must remain hard to beat!

Among the many shows that were held in the epidemic of international exhibitions of the 1880s, was one that brought C.B.Norton to his first controlling position. Although he had been Secretary to the Bureau of Revenue at Philadelphia, in 1876 it was the American Exhibition of the Products, Arts and Manufactures of Foreign Nations, held in Boston in 1883 that gave him his first chance as Secretary of the Organizing Committee. This event was somewhat unusual, having exhibits from forty countries but none from the host country. It was organized by a private company, without government help apart from some official contact with foreign participants. In 1884–85 the World's Industrial and Cotton Centennial Exposition was held in New Orleans which commemorated not only the centennial of the first shipment of a bale of cotton from America, but also the development of the whole of the Southern section of the United States. It had direct help from Washington in the form of a $1,000,000 loan, as well as a government display based on some of the material shown at Philadelphia eight years before. There was a separate women's exhibition building, and also 'The Exhibits of The Coloured Races'. Seventeen countries participated and the main building, which covered 33 acres, contained a machinery hall where 'from the galleries overlooking more than two miles of shafting could be seen driving every known character of machinery'. Such was the exhibition's appeal that a group of patriotic New Orleans citizens raised $175,000 and purchased the entire thing with the idea of keeping it open to the public. It re-opened during the summer of 1885–86 but by the end of its extended run had compounded a deficit of $250,000.

The exhibition epidemic continued to spread. The Cape Colony held the first South African International Exhibition in 1877 in Cape Town. Belgium and the Netherlands followed with exhibitions at Amsterdam in 1883 and in Antwerp in 1885 and Brussels in 1888. In 1886 Queen Victoria's Jubilee provided the excuse for many special exhibitions held throughout the British Empire. Among the largest of these in Great Britain were the exhibitions at Edinburgh, where there was a splendid reproduction of a section of Old Edinburgh, and London, where there was a similar one of Old London. Both full size models were complete with very carefully researched architectural detail and characters in the old costumes – although, like many future exhibition reconstructions, not always with the right accents! London's Colonial and Indian Exhibition, under the presidency of the Prince of Wales, and the management of Sir Cunliffe Owen, was held in the Royal Horticultural Society's Gardens behind the Albert Hall, and opened by Queen Victoria herself. Its collected exhibits and organization led to the founding of the Imperial Institute (on the site of the present Royal College of Art), which in its new guise of the Commonwealth Institute, is now located in a building in Kensington High Street, London.

CHAPTER SIX

Eiffel's Tower and Chicago's White City

Tired and worn with the wonders that crowd all the
                                        space of the Fair,
A dazed and bewildered Sightseer falls asleep in
                                the wicker wheel-chair.
But still all the sights and impressions have got
                        his poor head in a whirl, –
He sees in his dreams a wild jumble of it all
                                pass around in a swirl.
Haunted, pursued, persecuted, he dreams as they
                                wheel him away –
The fate of a man, flabbergasted, who tried 'to
                        see it all in one day'.

World's Fair Puck 1893, Anon.

As international exhibitions became a fashionable form of international public relations – indeed a mandatory exercise if the country was to be classed with the world powers – so it became less important to consider financial profit as one of the major motives. It was more important for each succeeding event to be seen as a greater, larger and more epic exhibition than the last, especially if the country holding it was indeed a world power.

In true public relations fashion, and usually to provide the increasingly necessary excuse for using such large sums of public money, it was also thought necessary to have some sort of historical or thematic reason for holding an international exhibition. The excuses, although often valid, like the celebration of the 400th anniversary of Columbus's landing in America in 1492, had often lost their sting by the time the event took place. This was because of the length of time taken to organize, plan and build international exhibitions, or because stronger commercial or design attitudes had obliterated the theme.

France was much surprised when her massive Exposition Universelle of 1889 actually made a small profit. Some nations had even expressed doubt about the wisdom of holding an international exhibition in Paris in 1889 at all! This was mostly because of the official reason for the event: the commemoration of the centennial of the French Revolution in 1789. Many foreign governments, especially the European monarchies, who were invited to participate were afraid that violent demonstrations and civil disorder would result and so did not exhibit officially.

56. Punch's view of M. Eiffel. Paris 1889. (*Punch* 1889)

Although the French President M. Carnot opened the Exposition in an atmosphere of ministerial, financial and anarchistic crises, in the event the fears were unfounded and the exhibition passed off peacefully; some people even considered that it had calmed the situation by providing an outlet for the energies of many of the likely troublemakers.

Once again the now traditional Champ de Mars site was used with the addition of more of the south bank of the Seine forming a link between the two areas – the Esplanade des Invalides. Two specially commissioned masterpieces were to tower over the site. One of these was pulled down in an act of 'artistic sadism' in 1910, the other still stands. It is the world's most photographed and illustrated exhibition structure and has become the international symbol of the City of Paris – the Eiffel Tower. It is now universally recognized and Paris would seem very unfinished without it but in 1885 when it was first proposed by Gustave Eiffel as a suitable symbol for the exhibition, it was anything but popular. The French Minister of Trade, who had given the go-ahead to the project and supplied a fifth of the estimated Fr27,500,000 cost, was swamped with complaints and petitions. None of these were as powerful in their hostility to *La Tour* as the writers and artists of Paris who, only a month after Eiffel had signed the contract, presented their long manifesto to M. Charles Adolph Alphand, the Director General of the Exhibition: 'We, the

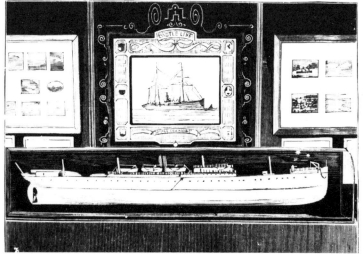

writers, painters, sculptors, and architects come in the name of French good taste and of this menace to French history to express our deep indignation that there should stand in the heart of our Capital this unnecessary and monstrous Tour Eiffel.' Eiffel however had put up the remaining four fifths of the money needed (mortgaging his company to do so), had spent two years working on its design with a staff of forty assistants and was not going to be put off. He remained completely unruffled and confident of the final outcome. 'When it's finished they will love it.'

Constructed from 15,000 wrought-iron sections, each precisely factory-made to Eiffel's highly detailed drawings, and fastened together with over 2,500,000 rivets, the tower rose steadily on its revolutionary reinforced-concrete foundations. By March 1889 the main structure was complete and on Sunday 31 March Eiffel and a small party of exhibition dignitaries climbed to the top of the tower with a small cannon to fire a twenty-one gun salute. Eiffel hauled the tricolour up announcing proudly that 'Now the French Flag is the

59. Ticket to the Exposition. Paris 1889. (*L'Exposition de Paris 1889*)

Opposite
57. Exhibits and Display cases in the unofficial British Section organized by the Lord Mayor of London. Paris 1889. (*L'Exposition de Paris 1889*)

58. Building the Exposition – the state of work in October 1888. Paris 1889. (*L'Exposition de Paris 1889*)

only one to have a nine hundred and eighty-four foot pole', a comment which summed up the sentiments behind the holding of the exhibition. Eiffel's contract with the French Government and the City of Paris gave him the revenue from all visits to the tower for the next twenty years. By May 1889 his investment was repaid and he found himself with a gold mine, one which was to get an added boost during the 1900 Exposition Universelle.

Local public reaction to the tower after it opened was varied: 'It's beautiful, it's great, it's sublime' . . . 'this dizzily ridiculous tower dominating Paris like a gigantic factory chimney' . . . 'the transformation of the techniques of architecture.' To visitors from abroad however, it remained a much admired and exciting structure, even if like George Hadfield they got lost on it: '. . . found myself waiting for ascent of Eiffel Tower. I took a ticket (3 frs) to second storey, going up, of course, by lift. After examining the splendid view there I paid another 2 francs to go up to the top. After ascending a certain distance the lift stopped and I thought we all alighted; I followed the crowd, entered another lift and to my astonishment found myself falling to the second étage! I must have made a great mistake as I ought still to have ascended. I did not find it out till back on the ground. I walked down the escalator from 2nd to 1st floor and was nearly terrified in the descent . . . the wind blowing hard and rain fast falling.' (1) It was to remain the world's highest man-made structure for forty years but was finally overtaken by the skyscrapers that Eiffel had helped to make possible through careful calculations on wind resistance and his awareness of and work on the effects of vertigo and gusting winds on the men involved in building at such heights.

The other great engineering masterpiece was Cotamin's Palais des Machines. Since Joseph Paxton had conceived the barrel transept of his Crystal Palace and the Palais de l'Industrie had overcome its roof loading problems with large blocks of lead, it had been

60. Erecting the exhibits in the Galerie des Machines. Paris 1889. (*Illustrated London News* 1889)

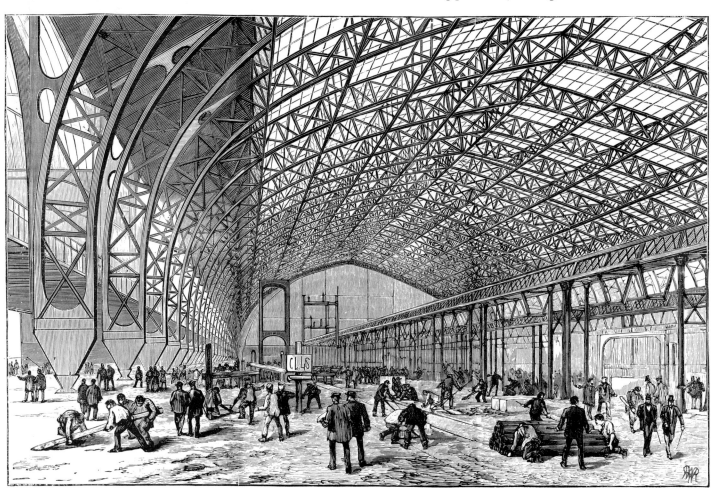

61. Les Ponts Roulants in the Galerie des Machines. Paris 1889. (*Illustrated London News* 1889)

the engineers' dream to find a way of covering the largest possible area of ground with the least number of roof supports. Railway architecture had provided the initiative between the great exhibitions and Barlow had produced the largest span to date with his design for St Pancras Station in London where the roof vaults were supported by heavy anchors and tie beams in the ground. Cotamin, however, was to balance his gigantic roof, like an elephantine ballet dancer on points, on huge hinged supports in the concrete foundation raft. The roof was also pivoted on a gigantic pin at the apex of each arch, thus allowing the great structure to take up the necessary amount of structural movement within itself. A great deal of it was made of steel and P. Morton Shand wrote of it 'Steel had found its form at last. Construction had once again become its own expression, its own "style". Cotamin's Galerie des Machines was one of the loveliest shapes in which man has ever enclosed space ; but whereas hitherto it has always been imprisoned like a bird in a cage, here it floated free as the circumambient air.' Eiffel's bridge over the River Doure in Portugal, which he built in 1875, had provided both Cotamin with information on the use of hinged joints and Eiffel with the necessary expertise for the construction of his tower. It reflected the close relationship between inventive structural engineering at that time and the application of such discoveries to building – a close link to which we have once more returned today after a period of academic building. Within the huge Galerie des Machines with its 375 foot wide central aisle were all the huge machines of industry, and overhead, like the one built into the 1878 Paris Exhibition's Machinery Gallery, was a giant travelling platform, Les Ponts Roulant, from which the visitors could look down on these modern marvels of science and invention. This exhibition also saw the advent of a new specialist in the engineering field – the electrician. The marvel that gave an ethereal dreamlike quality to

79

the whole Exposition after dark and provided much amusement and entertainment during the day was electricity. For the first time it was used throughout an international exhibition and it provided many of the best remembered moments, from the illumination of the Eiffel Tower and the glorious displays put on each evening by the fountain in the centre of the Champ de Mars (manually controlled using great railway signal box levers), to the individual excitement of the demonstrations of Mr Edison's telephone and phonograph, 'I applied Edison's telephonic apparatus to my ear and heard the band being played at a theatre near . . . quite clearly. Also in another machine I heard a solo sung by a man (which song had been bottled) . . . also very clearly.' (2)

In the special Pavilion de l'Aéronautique Militaire were the successors to the balloons used during the Siege of Paris in 1870, the early airships with their flimsy gas bags and even flimsier passenger baskets. There were captive balloons for the more adventurous visitors, and for those less disposed to viewing the show from such surroundings there were small balloons with special message cards which could be bought on the second floor level of the Eiffel Tower and dispatched to a friend or lover over the side of the tower.

62. Edison's Phonograph being demonstrated to the public in the Galerie des Machines. Paris 1889. (*L'Exposition de Paris 1889*)

Other things were to get dispatched over the side of the tower in the following decades. By 1970 over 350 people had jumped to their deaths from the tower which, despite elaborate precautions, has become Paris's favourite suicide leap. Apart from the grand exposition palaces with their statue-encrusted façades, there was a large colonial section with reproductions of native villages and parts of the great Angkor Wat Temple. Also nearby was a reconstruction of a Cairo street with native dancers doing their *danse du ventre* which was to cause such commotion in Chicago four years later. Amongst the more unusual exhibits were two thematic displays which carried on the tradition started at the 1867 Paris exposition. One of these, showing a complete full-size historical survey of human habitations, stretched across the whole width of the Champ de Mars in front of the Eiffel Tower. The other showed by means of a series of static model tableaux the development of work through the ages. Elsewhere in the exhibition much use was made of dioramas, panoramas and models to present ideas and views as diverse as the extraction of oil in the Russian steppes and a complete panorama of Paris herself. One of these spectaculars, which made use of photography to produce its effects, was the work of MM. de Neuville and Détaille and presented the Battle of Rézonville with the help of tall cylindrical mirrors.

An even more ingenious display was to be found in the Liberal Arts Palace where there was a great Terrestrial Globe: 'I ascended by lift to the top of the great globe and descended by an inclined plane running around the Globe! It was most interesting and instructive and I viewed objects of great interest, their name being legend. I am astounded!' (3) In the gigantic Central Palace built in front of the Galerie des Machines was a hint of the Art Nouveau style to come in the glassware exhibited by Emile Gallé of Nice. Across the Seine, completing the central Champ de Mars vista, was the Palais du Trocadero from the 1878 Exhibition with all the horticultural exhibits laid out on either side of the central fountains. In the Art Department, the Naturalists won the critical acclaim since the Impressionists were still officially ignored by the French Academicians. The paintings of the British artists Burne-Jones, Millais, Alma Tadema and Watts were especially praised.

The whole event, including as it did monumental theatrical performances by combined army and navy groups of 'L'Ode Triumphale de la République', was a festival for French republican politicians and well deserved its nickname of L'Exposition Tricolorée. Everyone was therefore much pleased as well as surprised when it was announced that it had made a modest profit.

The World's Columbian Exposition was another massive undertaking along the lines of the 1889 Paris Exposition and was to have as great an effect on America as it had on Chicago's Lake Michigan shoreline.

For some years past there had been much discussion in the columns of the press and in Congress in Washington as to how the 400th anniversary of Christopher Columbus's discovery of America in 1492 should be commemorated. It was finally decided that an international exhibition should form the centrepiece to the celebrations, but arguments over its location followed, and when Chicago was finally chosen time had run out and the project had to be moved forward to 1893, although the buildings were 'dedicated' in late 1892 to retain at least a little of the anniversary quality in the correct year!

If Paris 1889 was to be the apotheosis of the Victorian engineers with their structures, ingenuity and showmanship, Chicago in 1893 was to reflect all the worst traits of the academics who had been so opposed to Eiffel's Tower.

After extended discussions and inquiries the Exposition directors decided to locate the exhibition on the two pieces of South Park land fronting Lake Michigan and known as Jackson Park and Midway Plaisance. Jackson Park, in particular, was a very uninviting site consisting of a long strip of swampy sand ridges with a few clumps of scrub, with all the attendant wild life, including insects. However, the use of this unpromising land with an arrangement of ornamental lakes and canals and pavilions on the built-up land between (over 120,000 cubic yards of earth were moved in the process) gave the exhibition a character that was not to be repeated so successfully until Montreal's Expo 67.

Most of the international exhibitions had become so large that it was impossible to have the exhibits all in one main building and the attempt to do so in Paris in 1878 resulted in

81

EXPOSITION INTERNATIONALE DE LIÉGE 1930
AVRIL · NOVEMBRE
SOUS LE PATRONAGE OFFICIEL DU GOUVERNEMENT

PALAIS DE L'ÉLECTRICITÉ
(SECTEUR NORD)

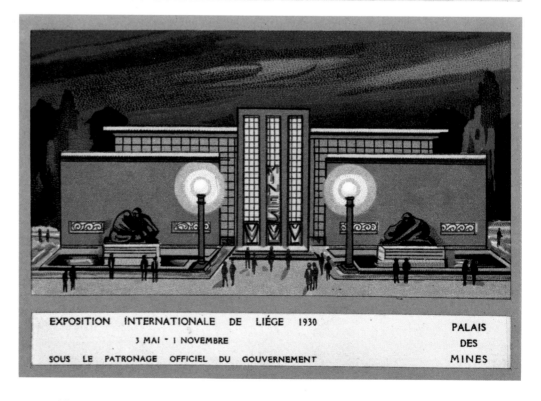

EXPOSITION INTERNATIONALE DE LIÉGE 1930
3 MAI · I NOVEMBRE
SOUS LE PATRONAGE OFFICIEL DU GOUVERNEMENT

PALAIS
DES
MINES

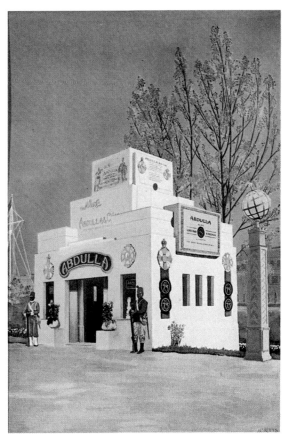

63. View North from Colonnade. Chicago 1893.
(*The White City (As it was)* 1893)

severe difficulties both for designers and visitors. Since then several buildings had normally been designed by different architects, resulting in various building styles. At Chicago one style was to dominate all the major buildings and a good few of the smaller ones as well – a style that split American architects into two distinct camps and made the President of the Exposition, Mr Thomas Palmer, state that looking at it 'a man can feel that he is in Athens during the age of Pericles.' It was officially called 'Neo-classical Florentine' and was to have a lasting effect on nearly all forms of American public and business architecture, especially banking, for a considerable period. It was also to affect future exhibition architecture and display well into the third decade of the next century. One of the 'new' group of architects whose revolutionary approach was virtually ignored was Louis Sullivan who foresaw the influence of the Exhibition and wrote one of the most quoted statements of American architectural criticism on the subject. 'Thus architecture died in the land of the free and the home of the brave – in a land declaring democracy, inventiveness, unique, daring enterprise, and progress. Thus ever works the pallid academic mind, denying the real, exalting the ficticious and false. The damage wrought by the World's Fair will last for half a century from its date, if not longer. It has penetrated deep into the constitution of the American mind effecting there lesions significant of dementia.' Vierendeel, a contemporary Belgian engineer, was also profoundly disappointed. 'The constructions were only imitations of what we have known in Europe for a long time. We expected better, much better, from the well-known audacity, initiative, and originality of the Americans. We have been profoundly deceived . . . In a new world they dared no innovations. They had doubts of themselves.'

84

The grand plan of the exhibition layout, which reflected the classical approach of the architecture, was designed by Frederick Law Olmsted who had done so much early work on the need for open spaces in modern city conurbations. From the beginning, it was based on the idea that all visitors on to the site entered through 'a great architectural court with a body of water therein; that this court should serve as a suitably dignified and impressive entrance hall to the Exposition, and that visitors arriving by train or by boat should all pass through it; that there should be a formal canal leading northward from this court to a series of broad waters of a lagoon character, by which the entire site would be penetrated, so that the principal Exposition buildings would each have a water, as well as a land frontage, and would be approachable by boats; that near the middle of this lagoon system there should be an island, about fifteen acres in area, that this island should be free from conspicuous buildings and that it should have a generally secluded, natural, sylvan aspect, the existing clusters of trees serving as centres for such broad and simple large masses of foliage as it would be practicable to establish in a year's time by plantations of young trees and bushes.' (4) Because the water in the lagoons would be subject to considerable fluctuations, it was also proposed that the shores should be occupied by a selection of such aquatic plants as would endure occasional submergence and yet survive an occasional withdrawal of water from their roots.

The final exhibition plan altered little from this original proposal and the visitors, having dropped their 50 cent ticket into the boxes at one of the turnstiles, passed into the great central entrance court seeing ahead of them what was considered by many to be the architectural masterpiece of the entire exhibition – the Administration Building. Perhaps in keeping with the falseness of the architecture, it contained few actual exhibits beneath its great golden dome. Although it looked very solid and strong, like the other buildings it

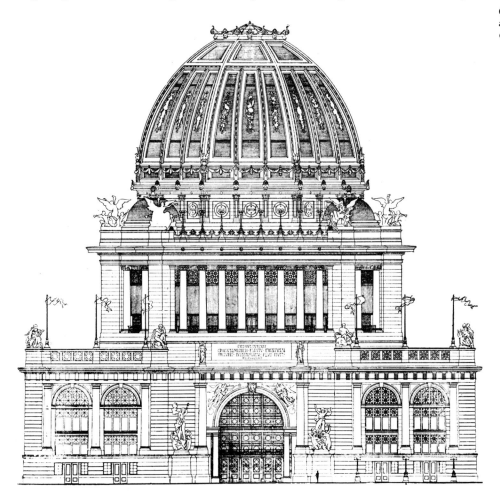

64. The Administration Building – an architectural elevation. Chicago 1893. (*World's Columbian Exposition Illustrated, 1891*)

was a wood and iron structure with the decorations and stone facings carried out in staff – a special mixture of plaster and cement with hemp and colouring pigments in it to represent white stone. Beneath the dome there were pictures and statues in the true neo-classical manner representing such values as Diligence, Abundance, Tradition, Liberty, Joy, and Patriotism as well as the Old World instructing the New World, carried out by Carl Bitters and his team of sculptors in yet more staff. All reflected an overall impression of what Hollywood directors and designers were tò cash in on just over twenty years later in their massive biblical and classical epics. The rest of the building merely contained the administration offices. To the rear of the great gold and white building was an immense basin of water fringed with balustrades, symbolic pillars, terraces and areas of grass and flower beds. In the foreground was a gigantic sculptural group by Frederick MacMonnie representing Columbia on her Ship of State being steered by Father Time, with the figure of Fame on the prow, all being driven through the water by eight girls standing at the oars, four on either side – a sight of such female supremacy that one chronicler of the Exposition, Mr Josiah Allen's Wife in the book *Samantha at the World's Fair*, was led to remark that she 'took it as bein' a compliment to me sect the way that fountain wuz laid out – ten or a dozen wimmen and only one or two men.'

At the outer end of the Grand Basin, with a 75 foot high golden statue of The Republic (very reminiscent of Bartholdi's Statue of Liberty in New York Harbour) was the great Columbus Memorial Arch forming the centre of a massive colonnade connecting the Music Hall and the Casino. Both identical in size and exterior architecture, the Music Hall and the Casino (which was filled with restaurants and rest rooms and not the gambling saloon its name might imply), formed the final gateway of the main vista out over the lake where there was a small harbour with a pier carrying the famous Movable Sidewalk. This would more correctly have been called a movable park bench, for it consisted of a procession of benches one behind the other. These were arranged on a series of low railway trucks with two platforms on them. The first of these moved at 3mph and was merely a stepping stone to the second which had the benches on it and moved at 6mph. The slower platform was directly mounted on the railway trucks whilst the faster platform ran on a second set of rails mounted on top of the trucks. The whole continuous line was powered by electricity and took the passengers out and back down the Casino Pier around a one-mile track under a covered awning. It was the first passenger-carrying platform to be built and was to be the forerunner of many such answers to the problems of tired and sore feet. It was only unfortunate that it should be tucked away in a rather obscure corner because the enormous tower feature that was going to be built at the end of the pier as a finale to the whole grand entrance court vista was never constructed.

The main means of transport was the intramural railway which circled the entire grounds. This was also an electric railway using a third-rail power source and was carried on an overhead structure. For 10 cents one could travel the whole distance in twenty minutes at a top speed of about 12mph. There were other more unusual means of transport available to the visitors including a Sliding Railway which operated on a water-lubricated central support rail and an Ice Railway which travelled on its 875 foot refrigerated ice base like a giant toboggan! As the *Shepp's World's Fair Photographed* wrote: 'Everywhere there is motion: electric launches, Gondolas, the Intramural Railway, the Sliding Railway, the Ice Railway, and the Movable Sidewalk; land and water alike are alive with happy people'. All the buildings around the great entrance court could be reached, as the planners had first envisaged, by either land or water. On the water there were electric launches, gondolas which had been brought over specially from Venice complete with their gondoliers, and larger steam launches which brought visitors direct from downtown Chicago right into the centre of the exhibition.

Within the palaces was a great wealth of exhibits. Most of the smaller items were shown in the traditional mahogany and glass display cases. Much of the actual display work was trophy building or the making of gigantic patterns using basically simple materials to produce designs, some suitable or some quite alien, to the basic product. Such displays included pictures and maps made from various seeds and plants, a full-sized elephant

65. Munson typewriter with 'interchangeable all-steel type-wheels capable of writing every language'. Chicago 1893. (*A Week at the Fair*, 1893)

66. 'A walnut elephant . . .' peanuts alternated with oranges and lemons to provide the detail on an elephant made of walnuts. Chicago 1893. (*The Magic City*, 1894)

carrying a houda completely constructed out of walnuts, and the familiar gold obelisk representing gold production, this time gracing Brazil's display.

Electricity was everywhere, lighting, pumping and driving. In the Machinery Hall many of the items were driven by electric power from the 127 dynamos in the adjacent Power House. The sheer size of the machinery developments since 1876 can perhaps be best underlined by the fact that whereas Corlis was the only American manufacturer of large engines in 1876, in 1893 there were sixty such American manufacturers alone, all producing engines far bigger and better than the 1876 one. So great was the impression of the machinery-in-motion display that a Turkish visitor was heard to remark 'Whiz, Whiz, all by wheels; whirr, whirr, all by steam', as he stood, eyes agog. The other main palaces, including those of Transportation, Horticulture, Fine Arts, Fisheries and the Women's Building were grouped, with the Mines, Electrical and Manufactures & Liberal Arts Buildings, around the lagoon with its wooded island in the centre where the Japanese *Ho-o-den* and tea garden, a reconstruction of a pioneer's log cabin, and the rose garden were exhibited. Further north were the pavilions of the foreign governments and the American

67. 'A Fair Warning' of the dangers of falling asleep in a Rolling Chair (*World's Fair Puck* 1893. Chicago Historical Society Collection)

68. Province of Ontario exhibit, Canadian section of the Agricultural Building. Chicago 1893. (*Shepp's World Fair Photographed*, 1893)

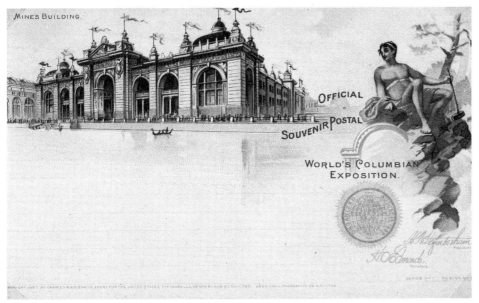

MINES BUILDING.

OFFICIAL
SOUVENIR POSTAL

WORLD'S COLUMBIAN
EXPOSITION.

69. Official Souvenir Postcard showing the Mines Building – one from a series of cards which formed America's first pictorial postcards (published by Charles Goldsmith). Chicago 1893.

States and to the South were the gigantic stock exhibits and the Forestry, Fishing and Farming displays.

The largest building contained the Manufactures & Liberal Arts which fronted the lake and covered nearly 30½ acres including a central span 7 feet greater than that at the 1889 Paris Exposition. Within were to be found all the manufactures of the world, everything from a sewing machine to a pin, from a watch to the giant alabaster clock built by the American Self-Winding Company as the building's centrepiece which, on its nine bells, reminded visitors to the building 'in notes of the sweetest music of the flight not only of the happy hours, but of the happy halves and quarters as well'. (5) All this could be viewed from the giant Otis elevators which took people up on to the flat roof of the building to look out over the site.

Although Sullivan is best remembered for his criticism of the Exposition architecture, he and his partner Adler designed the Transportation building with a great arched Golden Door decorated with allegorical figures and groups in bas-relief all covered with a thin layer of gold leaf. It was to be the only major building on the site which managed a valiant attempt against the Neo-Classical Florentine, and with its blatant colour scheme gave some of the critics at least a little hope of better things to come. Inside were all the latest transportation marvels, especially railways, from England, France, Germany, Canada, Mexico and America, with displays by the Pullman Company of their most luxurious New York & Chicago Limited Express coaches, the latest automobiles, and a full-size cross section of a modern transatlantic liner over four stories high and including a completely furnished interior based on the one shown at Paris in 1889.

Out on the waters of Lake Michigan were further transportation exhibits, amongst them a full-size replica of Columbus's flag ship, *Santa Maria*, which had been presented by the Spanish government and which sailed from Palos in Spain to the Exposition site with her sister ships *Nina* and *Pinta*. Beside the main Pier, where the steamers from downtown Chicago disgorged their visitors, was the United States Battleship *Illinois*. Although she stood 'grim and stern, white as though pale through long and arduous struggle with a desperate foe . . . turrets armed with formidable guns' (6) she was in fact, merely a replica built on piles driven into the lake bed. However, she was complete in every other way and matched the artificial façades and antique architecture of the rest of the exposition.

The Midway Plaisance had 'no connection with the Exposition proper excepting as side attractions'. (7) For small additional charges varying from 10 to 50 cents, these sideshows gave visitors the chance to view reproductions of Japanese, Irish, Javanese, German, Turkish, Moorish, Austrian, Dahoman, Lapland and Chinese villages as well as the famous Street of Cairo. Here amidst the hustle and bustle of the reconstructed scene was a theatre

Plate X
The *Chicago Daily News* 'Souvenir of a Century
of Progress, 1934' supplement. Chicago
1933–34. (*The Chicago Daily News*)

Plate VIII
'At night in the Grand Court' Chicago 1893. (*The
World's Fair in Water Colors* Graham, C., 1893)

Plate IX
South Tower, entrance to Homes and Gardens
Building, under floodlighting. San Francisco
1939–40. (*Treasure Island 'The Magic City'
1939–40*)

59TH YEAR. COPYRIGHT 1934 BY THE CHICAGO DAILY NEWS, INC   MAY 26—NOVEMBER 1   PHOTOGRAVURE ISSUE

THE NEW FAIR IN ALL ITS COLORS

THE SINGING FOUNTAIN, WHERE EACH CADENCE HAS ITS VIVID HUE
The Firestone Singing Fountain, with its color harmonies attuned to the musical scale, again will entertain exposition throngs at night. It occupies a court outside the enlarged Firestone building just north of 23d street.

THE ELECTRICAL BUILDING
At the left appears the water gate, with its two ornamental pylons 100 feet tall.
(Color photo by Harry Wells)

AN OLD MILL WITH ITS TRANQUIL POND
Only a few yards removed from busy world's fair boulevards is this scene of quiet rural beauty in the Horticultural gardens. A swan makes itself at home in the quiet waters. (Color photo by James H. Burdett)

THE GIANT NEW FOUNTAIN TWO BLOCKS LONG THAT FEATURES THIS YEAR'S FAIR
This great fountain two blocks long is the outstanding feature of A Century of Progress, 1934. Fanlike beams of colored light, similar to the '33 display at the south end of the grounds, give it a brilliant background. It extends southward into the north lagoon from the 12th street bridge. A mammoth dome of water plays at the lower tip.

IN THE GOLDEN PAVILION OF JEHOL
The Chinese Lama Temple with its statues of Buddha, rare carvings and red lacquer walls presents a vision of oriental splendor. Its original was built by Manchu emperors. (Color photo by Clyde T. Brown, staff photographer)

Opposite
71. The Ferris Wheel. Chicago 1893. (*The White City (As it was)* 1894)

70. The Golden Door of the Transportation Building by Louis Sullivan. Chicago 1893. (*The White City (As it was)* 1894)

where the American public was astounded by the 'genuine native muscle dance' of the Egyptian dancing girls. The belly dancing, which relied on maximum pelvic movement and minimum foot movement, came as a shock to the still puritanical American society, and certainly did not amuse everybody. 'The Cairo dancing was simply horrid, no touch of grace in it, only the most deforming movement of the whole abdominal and lumbar region. We thought it indecent'. (8) However it led to a national craze for the hootchy-kootchy, and was to be the basis for a tradition of sex-based sideshows at future American exhibitions – a tradition that can be traced back to a young stage singer, Bettina Ordway, who had secured useful publicity by the simple expedient, then thought very daring, of purchasing a diaphanous cotton nightgown at the Egyptian display in Philadelphia in 1876 and leaving it on display with her name embroidered on it!

Other attractions of the Midway Plaisance included the Libby Glass Company's and the Venice and Murano Company's glass factories showing the process of manufacture and selling the finished wares. The Hagenbeck Animal Show had tigers on velocipedes and pigs playing cards whilst the captive balloon took sixteen visitors at a time for rides up to a

72. 'There was one man who sells stoves who
has built a stove as big as a house . . . he asks
folks to step into the stove.' (*Samantha at the
World's Fair* by Joseph Allen's Wife. Dana Scott
Collection)

maximum height of 1,493 feet – the cost of $2.00 per ascent was also high. There was no
doubt however as to which exhibit was the most spectacular. Many suggestions had been
made for an exhibition feature to rival the Eiffel Tower, but the final answer was given by a
Mr G.W.G.Ferris of Pittsburg who suggested, carried out and paid for, a gigantic
revolving wheel 250 feet in diameter which would carry passengers. It was the original
Ferris Wheel. With its 36 cars each holding 40 passengers the 1,440 people were carried
round once every ten minutes, including the six stops made on each revolution to allow
people to join and leave the wheel – all for 50 cents, which soon returned Mr Ferris's outlay
of $400,000. Like Eiffel before him, he found himself making a fortune.

Today the big wheel is an important part of many fairs and the name given to Chicago's
amusement area gave American exhibitions the generic name for their amusement
sections: the Midway. In much the same way the popular name for the whole exhibition,
the White City, was also to be used by many future shows both in America and abroad.
There is now little left except the improved Chicago shoreline and the old Fine Arts
building which was reconstructed in limestone in 1928–32, and now houses Chicago's
famous Museum of Science and Industry.

On 10 July 1893 fire demolished the enormous Cold Storage House in the south-western
corner of the exhibition grounds and claimed the lives of sixteen firemen in the process.
Disaster in a more unexpected form was to strike again at the end of the Exposition.
Saturday 28 October had seen a large gathering of Mayors from all over America to say
farewell to the Exposition which was to close the following Monday. After the festivities
and speech-making the Mayor of Chicago, Carter Henry Harrison, returned to his home in
Ashland Boulevard and was shot dead by an assassin's bullets. As a result the Exposition
closed with a more than usually sombre official ceremony without any of the music,
speeches or fireworks that had been planned.

Some of the exhibits from Chicago were taken on to San Francisco so that people living
on the west coast could see the show. Suggested and organized by M. H. de Young, who
had been California's Commissioner and 2nd Vice-President of the Chicago Exposition, the
California Midwinter International Exposition opened on 27 January 1894 in San
Francisco's Piedmont Park, near the Golden Gate, with the elephant from Los Angeles
County in walnuts, the Firth Wheel, and a reconstruction of a '49 Mining Camp reflecting
'the days of old, the days of gold'. (9) Pan City, as it was nicknamed, was the first major
exhibition to reflect the 'neo-classical Florentine' style of Chicago and had its own
Administration building plus four other major exhibit buildings.

Not wanting to miss the exhibition bandwagon Jamaica held one of her own in 1891 in a
cream and red building north of the Kingston race course. Canada had the biggest foreign
display, having a special annex built alongside the exhibits of America, Britain,
Austria–Hungary, Italy, Surinam and the West Indian Islands. Further south an exhibition
on much the same lines as the Jamaican one was held in Guatemala City in 1897 when
France, Germany, Belgium, Italy and Chile were among the exhibitors.

Plate XI
Werner Luginbuhl's metal sculpture *The Bow* framing the Swiss, Austrian and 'Man the Explorer' theme pavilions. Montreal 1967. (Mary Allwood)

Plate XII
The Atomium at the head of the water ladder. Brussels 1958.

CHAPTER SEVEN
An Architectural Fantasia

. . . a new and ephemeral city hidden in the centre of the other, a whole quarter of Paris in fancy dress, a ball, where the buildings were the masqueraders. To our childish eyes it was a marvel, a coloured picture book, a cave filled by strangers with treasure.

Paul Morand, '1900 AD' (trans. Mrs Romilly Fedden)

'This will be the end of a century of prodigious scientific and economic effort. It will also be the threshold of an era whose actual achievements will doubtless surpass our wildest dreams.' Thus in the early summer of 1892 the Republic of France announced its intention of holding a great exhibition to welcome the new century, and thwarted the growing interest that Germany and the German Emperor were showing in holding what would have been the first German International Exhibition. Despite the brave showing of 1889, France was still feeling the humiliation of her 1870 defeat, and she was surprised by the response to the plan. Nations not only replied promptly, accepting the invitation to participate, but many immediately started planning their exhibits with evident enthusiasm.

Despite this initial interest and support, the exhibition was not to be a financial success. The optimism of the organizers had appeared to be justified – there were many original and inventive exhibits to attract the public, there was considerable foreign participation, and

74. *Le Pavillon Bleu* at the foot of the Eiffel Tower – the most fashionable restaurant at the exhibition. Paris 1900. (*L'Exposition du Siècle*, 1900)

73. A cancelled ticket to the Exposition. Paris 1900.

75. 'The Paris Room' in the Hamburg Museum
fur Kunst und Gewerbe. Director Julius
Brinckmann bought enough at the exhibition to
fill a whole room, including a Burne-Jones
tapestry, *The Adoration of the Magi*. Paris 1900.
(Hamburg Museum fur Kunst und Gewerbe)

the summer weather was the best Paris had had for many years. But the number of visitors fell short of those expected by nearly one third. The main reason for this was undoubtedly a monetary one. The high organizational and running costs were reflected in the cost to the visiting public. Calculations showed that a visitor would have to spend 600 francs over and above his entry ticket to see all the commercial attractions.

Rents for the leases of sites were very high, having been based on the expected attendance at the exhibition, and many of the concessionaires were soon in financial difficulties. (One restauranteur claimed that he needed to serve one million meals at 3.50–4.00 francs each just to break even. Needless to say, he did not get the chance to serve so many.) The resulting anger of the concessionaires, and their threats to strike eventually obtained for them a partial refund of the high fees they had paid.

When it closed after six months, the exposition had made a loss of 82,000 francs. The general public had lost money on the *bons* or shares they had bought to help provide capital, and for the first time in Paris, everyone was disheartened and disillusioned by the whole event. 'We'll have no more expositions. This is the last.'

And yet the organization for the exhibition had begun well. The traditional site was to be used, with an additional area on the right bank of the Seine, stretching over the land occupied by the 1855 Palais de l'Industrie and beyond to the Place de la Concorde. The Palais de l'Industrie was demolished, and in its place rose two buildings which still occupy the site, and are now used for conferences and major art exhibitions – the Grand Palais and the Petit Palais. A new bridge, the Pont Alexandre III, was specially built to link the Esplanade des Invalides with the new roadway between these two buildings, thus creating a second major vista on the exposition site. The Palais du Trocadéro from 1878 was retained, and also the great Galerie des Machines and the Eiffel Tower from 1889. The tower was the subject of many varied and strange schemes put forward by architects,

76. 'Vue Scénographique de L'Exposition Universelle de 1900' – a souvenir.

engineers, designers and eccentrics for either improvement or camouflage. In the event the only thing that altered was that the tower was given a new coat of golden yellow paint for the occasion. The Exposition's major buildings and features were nearly all designed by the architects of the École des Beaux Arts who carefully covered the engineering, which had been so obvious at the 1889 Exposition, behind false architectural stone façades.

It seemed that the old problem of transportation was to be partly solved. The Bateaux Mouches introduced in 1867 were still in use, and Paris was in the process of constructing the first line of her underground railway from Porte de Vincennes in the east, where a small industrial and agricultural annex to the Exposition was to be located, to Porte Maillot in the west; connecting the business centre of Paris with the then still remote exposition site, which had previously been served only by an infrequent horse-drawn omnibus service. Today the entrance gateways to the Metro, designed by Hector Guimard in the Art Nouveau style, are one of the most obvious reminders of a decorative style that was to reach its peak in France at the 1900 Exposition Universelle.

The style of Art Nouveau had been particularly noticeable in the glassware of Émile Gallé at the Paris Exposition eleven years before. Now it was to be used throughout the exposition, even reflected in the design of some of the buildings. Basically Art Nouveau was a break with the two major routes that Western art was then following – first the historical or academic approach, so evident in the architecture and planning of Chicago's World's Columbian Exposition, and secondly as a reaction against the popular naturalism, which even the academicians no longer favoured. It looked into the future for its inspiration, thus explaining the dreamlike and futuristic quality so evident in much of the work. The means and the end results varied enormously but usually had a fluid un-geometric quality. For the first time the fine arts were directly influenced by a style that started life in the applied arts, rather than the other way around. The true Art Nouveau artists considered that framed paintings were outside their terms of reference. They thought that fine art should be a direct extension of applied and useful art, and favoured the application of art as decoration to either a building or some other environmental object rather than letting the fine art be an object in its own individual right unconnected with its surroundings. The largest and most ostentatious Art Nouveau structure in the exposition was the Porte Monumentale which had been erected as the main entrance on the Place de la Concorde. René Binet's design for the three-legged arched dome was very reminiscent of the organic architecture of the Spaniard Antonio Gaudi, perhaps the most famous of the architects influenced by Art Nouveau. Parisians called the gate *La Salamanda* after the stoves so popular at the time, and levelled criticism at the statue of *La Parisienne* by Moreau-Vauthier which graced the top of the edifice. With her flowing robe and streamlined figure she was considered the last word in both modernity and bad taste, 'a triumph of prostitution'. Some gossips were even heard to remark that the model for it was the great Sarah Bernhardt herself, then fifty-five and still thrilling Paris with her performances as Napoleon's son in Edmond Rostand's *L'Aiglon*. The Grand Palais and the Petit Palais were outwardly in the academic style, but inside Art Nouveau ran riot, with beautifully curved iron galleries around the vast glazed hall of the Grand Palais, the wide generous sweep of the grand staircase of reinforced concrete, and the splendid iron entrance gates by Giraud in the Petit Palais.

Across the new Pont Alexandre III, with its sculptures designed by Jules Dalou, could be seen the sections of the exhibition concerned with the decorative arts, housed in two long symmetrical buildings, foreign exhibits on the right and French exhibits on the left, with the Hôtel des Invalides dome forming a finale to the complete vista. The buildings themselves were so covered in applied plaster decoration and of such complicated and convoluted shape that from a distance they gave the impression of many separate and highly decorated structures, rather than just two.

Within these palaces, the interior designers' productions reflected the Art Nouveau style, with a gigantic, if somewhat overweight, exhibit from Germany and a much prettier and more delicate exhibit from Austria, including work by Alfons Mucha, Josef Olbrich and Josef Hoffman. The French section was defeated by the method of display which, true to the old academic system of categories, decreed separate rooms for each type of exhibit, rather than showing the various objects in juxtaposition to each other in room settings. Only the pavilions of the great Paris department stores Le Printemps, Le Bon Marché, Le Louvre, and particularly M. Samuel Bing's pavilion designed by Georges de Feure displayed the whole range of European Art Nouveau products in close proximity.

In contrast, the British Royal Pavilion created by Sir Edwin Lutyens was an almost exact reproduction of The Hall at Bradford-on-Avon, Wiltshire. Far from being a public exhibition pavilion, it set out to provide the Commissioner with an Englishman's Castle on the site, much to the annoyance of many of the foreign visitors, especially the French hosts, 'The English, puffed up with pride, are afraid that not many people will visit their pavilion ... They have put an attendant in front of the closed door. The attendant says the door will shortly be opened, the crowd gathers, and there are people naïve enough to queue. This trick is often used by dentists.' (1) Although it was built to give the impression that it was constructed from permanent building materials, it was completely removable, being made from interlocking sheets of steel which were covered by a roughened cement made with crushed stone. Even the interior panelling could be taken apart and re-assembled elsewhere. The various rooms showed the great periods of English interior decoration, complete with an Art Nouveau main bedroom by the ecclesiastic craftsmen and women of the Bromsgrove Guild of Applied Art!

The Entente Cordiale was going through a particularly severe test at the time with all but one of the Paris newspapers actually being paid by the Boers to print anti-British propaganda and with Queen Victoria the butt for many cartoons and satires. The British Royal Commission's Report tactfully pointed out there were even areas where the host country appeared to be biased against the English in its use of the exposition's regulations, 'Certain classes of exhibits were transferred to Vincennes; but the Commissioners observe that, notwithstanding the assurances given to them by the Administration respecting the entire transfer of those classes, most of the French automobiles and cycles, and a considerable part of the French rolling stock for light railways and tramways, which were included in those classes, were shown on the Champ de Mars'. (2) Even the rule that the Fine Art exhibits must have been produced since May 1889, which was faithfully kept to by the British Commissioners, was 'not strictly followed in the French and foreign sections' reported the London *Times*.

The American pavilion, a pure piece of Chicago neo-classicism, became a base for American visitors rather than a display of exhibits, 'one well-equipped post office and you have seen America'. (3) Problems had arisen when it was discovered that the French organizers, by some oversight, had placed it in the second row of foreign pavilions and not

77. La Rue des Nations along the left bank of the River Seine. Paris 1900. (*Exposition Universelle, Paris 1900, Héliotypies de E. Le Deley*)

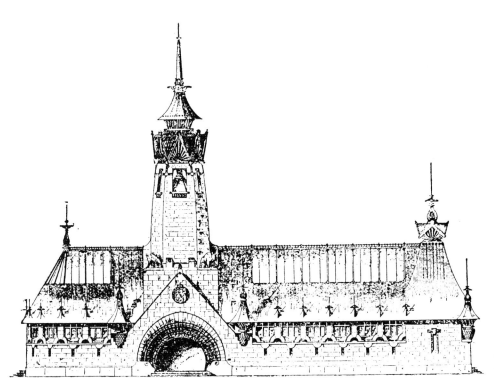

along the bank of the Seine. There followed much diplomatic activity and argument before each country already in the front line give up a little of its space and the American pavilion was squeezed in! The Americans spent more on their participation than any other country, (although much of the money went on the high transport costs), and were of great interest to the French visitors who had seen little of the new country and its tobacco-chewing, maize-eating inhabitants.

The most revolutionary building along the Rue des Nations, especially when compared with so many over-decorated exteriors, was the Finnish pavilion. Designed by Eliel Saarinen, father of the famous designer and architect, Eero Saarinen, its simple lines and careful details set it apart. The Swedish pavilion also stood out with its yellow paint and natural red deal structure covered with pine shingle-boards. It resembled a great galleon about to launch itself into the River Seine.

All the national pavilions were paid for, designed and even constructed in many cases, by the countries concerned. Each had been allocated its site by the French organizers, who usually had little control, and often scant knowledge, of what each country was going to produce. Problems were bound to arise. In later years whole pavilions were to be dominated or ruined by their neighbours – the Canadian pavilion at Brussels in 1958 suffered this fate when it was completely overpowered by the massive architecture and high blank wall of the Russian Cinema building, a fact that the Canadians did not discover until it was too late to alter their planning. The virtually unplanned foreign section at Paris in 1900 produced a splendid fantasia of national architectural styles, finishes and effects along the right bank of the Seine.

It was electricity once more that provided much of the interest and invention. The power was generated inside the Palais de l'Electricité in front of the Galerie des Machines, where visitors could see the great steam-driven dynamos pumping life into the whole exhibition. The front façade of this pavilion formed a major portion of the finale to the grand vista down the Champ de Mars under the Eiffel Tower: 'At night the whole façade is illuminated with the changing lights of its 5,000 multicoloured incandescent lamps, its eight monumental lamps of coloured glass, the lanterns of its sparkling pinnacles and its phosphorescent ramps. At the top the Spirit of Electricity, driving a chariot drawn by hippogryphs, projects showers of multicoloured flames. At night the openwork frieze forms a luminous embroidery of changing colours. The Palace of Electricity contains the living, active soul of the Exhibition, providing the whole of this colossal organism with movement and light . . . Without electricity the Exhibition is merely an inert mass devoid of the slightest breath of life . . . From the basement of the Palace leading in all directions, run miles and miles of wire transmitting power and light, along the walls, winding underground and crossing the Seine. A single touch of the finger on a switch and the magic fluid pours forth; everything is immediately illuminated, everything moves. The 16,000 incandescent lamps and the 300 arc-lamps light up at the same time, at the Porte Monumentale, and the Pont Alexandre III, in the Champs Élysées, at the Invalides, on the Champ de Mars and at the Trocadéro; The Chateau d'Eau sets its cascades of fire streaming. Everywhere the soul of the Palace of Electricity brings light and life'. (4) There were problems to start with and the exhibition was plunged into darkness and stillness once or twice but by the second week, when the weather also improved, all the hitches had been ironed out and people crowded in every evening to see the programme of water and light on the Chateau d'Eau. Others dined at the restaurant opposite the Palais Lumineux, a Chinese-inspired folly on a man-made hill in the gardens on the Champ de Mars illuminated by another display of light and water making full use of coloured beads and filters in front of the lamps.

In her own theatre on the site, an American, Loie Fuller, danced in the light of electric arc lamps and with her flowing veils and coloured lights brought the Art Nouveau female figure to life. The new display techniques included the introduction of some of the

79. La Porte Monumentale Paris 1900.
(*Exposition Universelle, Paris 1900, Héliotypies de E. Le Deley*)

80. 'Showing how the three speeds of the Trottoir Roulant correspond to the three ages of Life'. Paris 1900. (*L'Exposition de Paris 1900*)

forerunners of today's audio-visual extravaganzas. One of these designed by Raoul Grimoin-Sanson, a French inventor of early motion picture equipment, could easily have been the sensation of the whole Exposition. Unfortunately the projectors' arc lamps and the lack of ventilation, coupled with the highly inflammable film stock, caused the exposition authorities to shut it down after only three days, bringing to an end overnight three years of extremely hard work. The ten synchronised 70mm projectors produced a 330° picture closely resembling the modern *Circarama* of Walt Disney and the *Kinopanorama* later developed by the Russians. It was subsequently patented as *Cinéorama*. Unlike many other new inventions, it had a particularly imaginative programme to offer its 200 viewers. Grimoin-Sanson described the whole concept of his exhibit, 'I had made plans for a vast marquee containing white walls, a hundred metres in circumference, which would serve as an uninterrupted screen. In the centre was to be positioned the huge nacelle of a balloon equipped complete with anchor, ropes, ballast and ladders, and underneath this would be located ten projectors synchronized to a central motor. From the ceiling, curtain material would be draped to represent perfectly the casing of the balloon. When the audience have assumed their places in the nacelle, the lights would be dimmed for the commencement of the journey . . . leaving Paris, the balloon will travel around visiting Brussels, London, Barcelona and Tunis. The films projected on the walls depict scenes from these various cities, thereby creating the illusion of a tour of the capitals . . .' Jules Verne's *Round the World in Eighty Days* had quite possibly been a strong influence on Grimoin-Sanson.

This imaginative exhibit, with its handcoloured films, phonograph music and live commentary, was to be the first of many major developments in film technique and presentation which have had their first public showing at world exhibitions. Although not so creative, there were other audio-visual programmes, including three talkies although the phonograph sound and film vision were not too successfully synchronized. Amongst the best known of these was Clement Maurice's Phono-Cinéma-Théâtre with its short scenes including Sarah Bernhardt in *Hamlet*, Coquelin Ainé in the duel scene from *Cyrano*

81. Section through the Trottoir Roulant showing how the platforms ran on rails. Paris 1900. (*L'Exposition du Siècle*, 1900)

103

82. The timber Swedish pavilion between the Monaco and Greek pavilions on the Quai des Nations. Paris 1900. (*Exposition Universelle, Paris 1900, Héliotypies de E. Le Deley*)

de Bergerac and Little Tich in part of his Music Hall turn.

Elsewhere in the exhibition, and four years before Hale's Famous Tours programmes with their railcar auditoriums in America, there was the Maréorama with its heaving viewing platform built like the deck of a steamship (so successful many of the visitors were seasick). Its painted background, almost half a mile long, wound past the viewer from one enormous roller to the other, giving the impression of a voyage across the Mediterranean from Marseilles to Algiers in a storm.

There were some novel answers to the question of transport around the site. Following the lead set by the Moveable Sidewalk at Chicago, the Paris Exposition offered the Trottoir Roulant where 50 centimes paid for travel along a circular route connecting the Champ de Mars with the Esplanade des Invalides. It became one of the main attractions of the exhibition, rivalling even the Eiffel Tower. Devised by the team of Blot, Guyenot and de Mocomble, the Trottoir consisted of three concentric platforms. The first was fixed and

static serving as a stepping off point at the various stations along the route. The second moved at a speed of 2.25mph, and the third at a speed of 4.50mph. Unlike the Chicago experiment there were no chairs on the third platform – only posts to hang on to. However, riding on the Trottoir became so popular that seats were fitted during the exposition's run. The safety record was excellent – even allowing for the fine summer of 1900 (there was no awning except at the stations!) and the crowds of visitors with ladies in their long dresses, there were only forty minor accidents. The Paris newspapers were impressed: 'A railway without weight, noise or smoke; without cinders, smells or jars; where crowding and waiting is unknown; on which passengers cannot be knocked down by cars or have their legs cut off by wheels; on which there is no switching or obstructing of trucks, no delays at stations and on which collisions are made impossible . . .' (5) Unfortunately the costs of the experiment were not covered by the receipts.

In the large exhibition palaces were twenty-seven chemin élévateurs which carried

84. 'Dreamland' in the Midway – 'a blamed
puzzlin show, and thet big gal's face is mighty
appropriate, for females as a rool is puzzlin
critters'. Buffalo 1901. (*The Pan-American and
its Midway*, 1901)

visitors up on to the galleries of the pavilions. There were three basic types of escalator, all
using flexible belts rather than the steps we now expect.

In 1900 Paris also became the first place outside Greece to host the modern Olympic
Games. Although much smaller and with far fewer competitive events than today, the
Games were seen by the organizers as a part of the overall plan to make the scope of their
exhibition complete. The events were held at the annex at Vincennes, but the
arrangements were far from satisfactory – an American entrant threw his hammer about
130 feet but was disqualified because it hit a tree. Competition winners were given tie-pins
and pencils, plus 100 francs from which they were supposed to buy their own medals.
Needless to say few did!

On 22 September one of the more bizarre events of the exposition was held: the Banquet
des Maires. The French President, M. Loubert, and 20,777 Mayors from the largest cities to
the smallest hamlets sat down to a dinner prepared in eleven kitchens, served at 606 tables
and supervised by means of both telephone and autmobile. For a long time afterwards it
was to be seen as a further demonstration of the unity and success of the French Republic.

Together with the architectural legacy of Chicago, electricity also provided the
inspiration for the Pan-American Exposition held in Buffalo in New York State in 1901.
The abundant power from the Niagara Falls' hydro-electric scheme made the 389 foot
Electric Tower, designed by an architect, J. G. Howard, the central feature of the
exposition. Over 200,000 other lights, many of which were specially made non-dazzle
eight watt lamps, were used to outline the architectural form of the buildings, and to float

in the ceremonial fountain. Unlike Chicago, the Exposition was by no means a White City. The colours used on the buildings of this 'Rainbow City' were copied from Central and South American designs, and were bright, even gaudy. The Temple of Music, for example, was painted in bright red and salmon pink. Most buildings, as befitted their Spanish origins, also had red tiled roofs. The exposition grounds were symmetrically laid out round a T-shaped esplanade complete with two bandstands (very reminiscent of Binet's Porte Monumentale in Paris) and a cascade which was a forerunner of those to be built at St Louis three years later. It was the proud boast of the organizers that this esplanade could hold up to 250,000 people, although it was never put to the test.

But it seems to have been the Midway with all its razzmatazz that caught the public's imagination. Here were to be found the 700 representatives of the Indian Congress, amongst them Geronimo, held for fourteen years a war prisoner of the United States and now put on display by his own country alongside such spectacles as 'the Educated Horse' and 'Chiquita – the doll lady', a 26in. high 18lb. Cuban midget.

Among the exhibit pavilions, the most popular were the Machinery and Transportation Building with its automobile display, and the Liberal Arts Building which had a considerable number of food exhibits where free samples were available and where the pork dealers proudly advertised: 'Nothing lost but the squeal'.

The exhibition had originally been conceived as a gigantic trade fair to be held on Cayuga Island near Niagara Falls. The outbreak of the Spanish–American War in 1898 caused a postponement, and on the resumption of planning there was great competition between Niagara and Buffalo to be chosen as the exhibition site – a battle which was won by Buffalo on the merits of its size and existing communications, especially railroads. From the start it was partly financed by a $500,000 grant from Congress in Washington which wanted to see much closer relations between the countries of North, South and Central America. The Pan-American Exposition is unfortunately best remembered for the appalling tragedy that occurred at 4.07pm on Friday, 6 September 1901. President MacKinley had intended to visit the fair earlier but his wife's illness had made him change his plans. At the end of a three day visit to Buffalo and Niagara he returned to the Exposition grounds for a public reception at the Temple of Music which was to be the last official engagement of his visit. It was the last official engagement of his life.

He had evolved a method of shaking hands with up to forty-five people per minute and had just patted a small girl on the head and was stretching his hand out to the blue-eyed, boyish-faced man following her in the line-up, when there were two muffled shots. Leon Czolgosz had fired at point blank range. By six o'clock the President had undergone surgery and one of the bullets that had lodged by his breast bone had been removed. The other had penetrated his stomach and could not be found. Early on the morning of 13 September the President's condition worsened and after nearly twenty-four hours of fighting for his life he died at 2.15am on Saturday 14 September 1901.

The Exposition, which had been closed on the day of MacKinley's death, re-opened two days later but never really recovered from the blow dealt by Czolgosz.

Today the only remaining building in Delaware Park is the New York State Building. This now houses the Buffalo and Erie County Historical Society which still has the original architect's model of the Electric Tower amongst its archives.

Glasgow's Kelvingrove Park was the site of another international exhibition in 1901. Held to commemorate the jubilee of the Great Exhibition, it showed a substantial profit of £30,571, and attracted twice as many visitors as 1851.

It is interesting to conjecture what Charles Rennie Mackintosh would have made of the main exhibition building. Unfortunately he was not invited to submit a design, and Glasgow, with one of the leading exponents of Art Nouveau in her midst, managed to produce a very mundane building which had even less to offer than Captain Fowkes's 1862 design. Visitors passed through the grand entrance and beneath the great central dome, with its biblical quotations and names of famous Scottish inventors, and its twice life-size statue of the newly enthroned King Edward VII, to view the rows of giant steam locomotives and the myriad exhibits from the colonies and foreign countries. Outside there

85. 'How your feet feel at the end of the day'. Buffalo 1901. (*Around the Pan with Uncle Hank*, 1901)

86. The Grand Palace with female figures designed by Dubino. Turin 1902. (*Turin International Exhibition 1902 Commemorative Album*. Royal Society of Arts Collection)

was a reconstruction of a Russian village, a massive circular Concert Hall, which was used for the opening ceremonies, and boating on the River Kelvin to amuse and delight the crowds.

The profits of the 1888 Glasgow Exposition, together with money raised by the Art Gallery Building Fund Appeal, was used to erect the new Art Gallery and Museum in Kelvingrove Park in time for the 1901 Exposition. It housed a retrospective exhibit of nineteenth century art which included architecture and photography, as well as fine arts. There was also the nucleus of the museum collections with a chronological display on Scottish history including such things as highland games and Scottish customs.

If Glasgow could offer no adventurous Art Nouveau architecture, the Turin International Exposition of 1902 certainly could! From the massive entrance to D'Aronco's Grand Palace, with groups of cavorting females outside and organic Art Nouveau forms inside growing up to support the roof with its large clerestory windows, all the pavilions reflected the style in their architecture as well as their exhibits.

Scotland exhibited separately from the rest of Britain – Charles Rennie Mackintosh with his wife Margaret Macdonald-Mackintosh and their friends Jessie King, Herbert McNair and others, produced a display of furniture, fabrics and metalwork that in some small way helped to make up for the lack of inspiration of the Glasgow Exhibition the year before.

England was represented mainly by the Arts and Crafts Exhibition Society of London which showed work by William Morris, Walter Crane, C.F.A.Voysey, Philip Webb and

C.R.Ashbee, among others. France, with work by Lalique and de Feure, and Belgium, with work by Van de Voorde and Dubino, represented the more poetic organic Art Nouveau. In contrast, the fountain guarded by the wings of Peter Behrens' two angels, standing in the entrance foyer of the German pavilion displayed a much heavier and more solid approach once more.

The only non-European exhibitors were Japan, the source of much of the original impetus to the whole Art Nouveau movement, and America with designs by Louis Tiffany, including some of his famous electric lamp standards and shades.

In 1902–1903 there was a colonial-based exhibition in Tonkin (now Hanoi) in what was then French Indo-China. Organized to display the products, agriculture and industries of France's Far-Eastern colonies, the exhibition also had exhibits from Japan, China, Siam, Korea, and the Philippines as well as the French colonies in Africa. It even boasted a specially-built Palais des Beaux-Arts based on those at the Paris Exposition.

88. Stencilled banner designed by Charles Rennie Mackintosh for the Scottish Pavilion at the 1902 Turin International Exhibition. (University of Glasgow Collection)

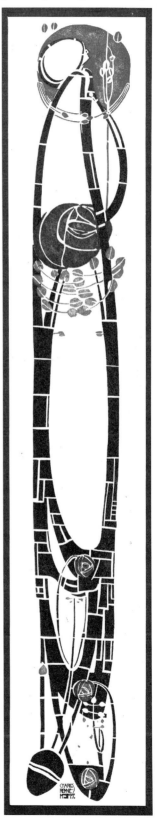

87. Souvenir plate. Glasgow 1901.

CHAPTER EIGHT

The Louisiana Purchase Exposition and Two Great Fires

Immensity is not the strongest claim to public interest.

Official publicity brochure, The Louisiana Purchase Exposition, 1904

It was bigger in area than the Philadelphia Centennial, the Chicago World's Columbian, and the Buffalo Pan-American Exhibitions added together. In fact all the exhibition buildings at Buffalo would have fitted into the Palace of Agriculture, which alone covered almost twenty acres. It had fifteen mammoth exhibition Palaces: 'veritable Golcondas of wealth and treasure'. It had the Olympic Games. It had all the American States and thirty-four foreign nations exhibiting. The Louisiana Purchase Exposition of 1904 was, in fact, bigger and better than any before it.

It was held to commemorate the Louisiana Purchase of 1803 when President Thomas Jefferson, unbeknown to the American Senate, bought Louisiana for $16,000,000, or 4 cents an acre, from Napoleon and increased the size of America by 140% overnight, but the Exposition was one year late. It had been instigated at a special convention held in 1899, and the site that was chosen was the largest and wealthiest city in the area, St Louis. Today, except within the vicinity itself, the Exhibition is all but forgotten. Forgotten, that is, except for a popular song:

> Now Louis came home to the flat,
> He hung up his coat and his hat,
> He gazed all around,
> But no wifey he found,
> So he said, 'Where can Flossie be at?'
> A note on the table he spied,
> He read it just once, then he cried.
> It ran, 'Louis dear,
> It's too slow for me here,
> So I think I will go for a ride.
> Meet me in St Louis, Louis,
> Meet me at the Fair,
> Don't tell me the lights are shining
> any place but there ...' (1)

The Universal Exhibition of 1904 was opened by President Theodore Roosevelt from the East Room of the White House in Washington – over 700 miles away. At 2.15pm on 30 April, surrounded by a large and impressive gathering of dignitaries, the President duly touched the special gold telegraph key (which had been used to open the Chicago Exhibition in 1893) and declared the exhibition open. On receiving the signal from Washington David R. Francis, the Exposition President lifted up his hands and also declared the exposition open. His speech concluded with the following words: 'Open ye gates! Swing wide ye portals! Enter herein ye sons of men! Learn the lesson here taught and gather from it inspiration for still greater accomplishments!' Ten thousand flags fluttered from their masts, the fountains under the Festival Hall shot into life and sent their torrents down the three gigantic cascades into the Grand Basin, the mighty machinery started and 200,000 voices and scores of bands declared the exhibition well and truly open.

Unlike the 1900 Paris Exposition, there was no lack of space, and the organizers had spread themselves over the available 1,272 acres, even making the great transverse Louisiana Way 30 feet wide. This gave the visitor a considerable walk from one pavilion to another – in fact the distance around the whole exhibition was 35 miles – and exhibition

Opposite
89. French Poster designed by Alphonse Mucha for the Lousiana Purchase Exposition. St Louis 1904. (St Louis Art Museum Collection – Gift in memory of David R. Francis, President, Lousiana Purchase Exposition, 1904, by his granddaughter, Miss Alice P. Frances)

RÉPUBLIQUE FRANÇAISE
MINISTÈRE DU COMMERCE DE L'INDUSTRIE DES POSTES ET TÉLÉGRAPHES
EXPOSITION UNIVERSELLE & INTERNATIONALE
DE St LOUIS (ÉTATS-UNIS)
DU 30 AVRIL AU 30 NOVEMBRE 1904.

DE PARIS A St LOUIS
6 JOURS DE STEAMER
ET 1 JOUR DE CHEMIN DE FER

Pour renseignements et adhésions concernant la FRANCE s'adresser au Ministère du Commerce,
Commissariat Général du Gouvernement Français, *101, Rue de Grenelle, PARIS,* et au Comité
de la Section Française à la Bourse du Commerce de PARIS.

IMPORTANCE DE L'EXPOSITION

PHILADELPHIE	1876	95 HECTARES	CHICAGO	1893	240 HECTARES
PARIS	1900	135 HECTARES	St LOUIS	1904	500 HECTARES

IMP. F. CHAMPENOIS _ PARIS

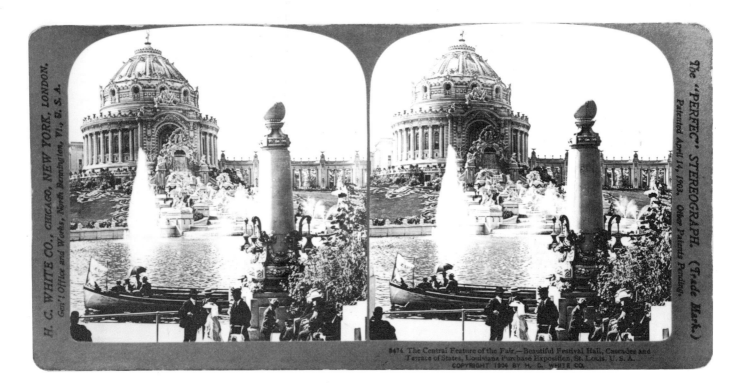

6476 The Central Feature of the Fair.—Beautiful Festival Hall, Cascades and
Terrace of States, Louisiana Purchase Exposition, St. Louis, U. S. A.
COPYRIGHT 1904 BY H. C. WHITE CO.

90. 'The Central Feature of the Fair – Beautiful
Festival Hall, Cascades and Terrace of the
States'. St Louis 1904. (*The 'Perfec' Stereograph*
by Messrs H. C. White & Co.)

organizers, if not architects in general, finally realized the advantages of a compact site
more related to human proportions.

The main palaces were located in the north-east corner of the site fanning out from the
Festival Hall, with its colonnades representing the Louisiana States and Territories. The
other two main buildings, the enormous Palace of Agriculture and the smaller Palace of
Horticulture with its 100 foot diameter floral clock, were located to the west of the main
group.

Architecturally the main exhibition palaces were almost identical to those at Chicago
and completely white. Structurally they differed in that wood was used instead of steel for
their framework. They were supported by sculptural decoration similar to that used in
Chicago, and the popular nickname, the Ivory City, given to the exhibition echoed the
nickname of White City given to the World's Columbian Exposition.

Within the main palaces were many thousands of exhibits ranging from one of the
largest agricultural displays ever assembled, which required a nine mile walk to view it, to
160 automobiles driven by petroleum, electricity or steam. One of these cars even drove to
St Louis from New York – a much admired feat. It was in the exhibiting of three wonders of
scientific achievement that St Louis excelled over Chicago. These were automobiles,
wireless and aeronautics.

While many hundreds of people daily viewed the latest automotive marvels in the
Palace of Transportation, great strides were being made on site in the field of wireless
telegraphy. When the exhibition opened, people queued up to send messages by wireless
from one side of the grounds to the other but by the time it closed seven months later
messages were being transmitted to Chicago over a distance of 250 miles. Amongst the
radio exhibits was Lee DeForest's valve which was to play a vital role in the future of
wireless.

In the eleven acre Aeronautics Field were balloons, flying machines, kites, aeroplanes, a
gliding machine and airships which had entered for the competitions suggested by the
Director of Exhibits, F.J.V.Skiff, and organized with the help of Santos Dumont, the
famous French flyer. Dumont's airship, *Number Seven*, was the largest contestant for the
main $100,000 prize for 'aeronautic achievement considerably beyond anything yet
attained' but unfortunately the envelope of his airship was maliciously slashed the night

after it was unloaded from its crate and Dumont had to withdraw from the contest. Although not meeting the contest regulations, Captain Baldwin's airship *California Arrow* made the first successful American dirigible flight from the exhibition ground on 25 October 1904. A tetrahedral kite sent by Professor Alexander Graham Bell was also demonstrated to the crowds during October.

Weil's special Exposition Band and fourteen guest bands, including John Philip Sousa's, the British Grenadier Guards, and the Garde Républicaine provided continuous music on the exhibition grounds. Some governments also sent their own bands, including the Mariachi Band from Mexico, the beginning of a tradition that has continued at all subsequent international exhibitions at which Mexico has exhibited. Other musical events ranged from the Berlin Philharmonic Orchestra to concerts on the great Festival Hall organ with its 10,059 pipes and 140 stops, and even included choral contests with $16,000 in prize money.

The pavilions erected by the American States and Territories provided a transition from the architectural dignity of the official Exhibition Palaces to the gaiety of the amusement area with the Lone Star Plan building of Texas and Tepee-like building of Washington State setting the scene for the showmanship, colour and Art Nouveau decoration elsewhere. Within, the States had much to offer the visitor including bizarre monuments created from household commodities like Louisiana's statue in sugar, and Pennsylvania's inevitable Liberty Bell.

Many of the visitors must have enjoyed the rich displays of architecture and heritage in the thirty-four foreign pavilions. Most countries built copies of their famous buildings or amalgams of a number of such structures. France had a replica of the Grand Trianon at Versailles, Britain had Wren's Kensington Palace Orangery. Belgium had the Old Town Hall of Antwerp – an interesting project from the exhibition designer's point-of-view as it

91. The Art Palace – official souvenir postcard. St Louis, 1904.

OFFICIAL SOUVENIR
WORLD'S FAIR- ST. LOUIS 1904

Art Palace.

SAMUEL CUPPLES ENVELOPE CO. ST LOUIS MO. SOLE WORLDS FAIR STATIONERS

113

92. Official advertising stickers:
a) Exposition Universelle Liège, 1905
b) Exposition Universelle et Internationale, Brusselles, 1910
c) Exposition Universelle et Internationale Gand, 1913

had no windows. China, exhibiting for the first time at a world exhibition, reproduced Prince Pu Lui's Summer Palace decorated with over 6,000 pieces of handcarved wood and India showed numerous pierced marble screens. The Siamese exhibits were displayed in a reproduction of one of the temple buildings from the Imperial Palace in Bangkok, a practice repeated in many exhibitions since, including Osaka in 1970. Some of these buildings contained elaborate exhibits, while others, like Canada's ornate pavilion, were only used for receptions and as headquarters for the national contingent.

The grouping of such diverse architectural styles was not universally admired, and many exhibition organizers planned their building styles and layouts more carefully. Even the large Panama-Pacific Exposition in San Francisco in 1915 was to have its main exhibition buildings carefully designed and planned as a homogeneous group, with the less easily controlled state and foreign pavilions placed to one side where they could not spoil the overall effect, whatever their appearance.

Like countless American country fairs since 1904, the amusement area was called The Pike. Apart from their national pavilions, many countries had also constructed native village settings along its length. There were vendors and dancing girls from 'The Streets of Cairo'; Igorrots from the Philippines; Eskimos from northern Canada; Japanese Aborigines; Workmen from China; even 1,000 natives imported to give the massive eleven-acre Jerusalem concession its character. But most interesting of all was the living ethnological exhibit in the Hall of Anthropology which contained everything from giants from Patagonia to pygmies from Africa. In fact between 15,000 and 20,000 people actually lived on the site during the exhibition. The health of these 'people of all climes and of varying degrees of civilisation from savage to enlightened' (2) had been of some concern to the organizers but the strict enforcement of health regulations stopped any contagious diseases gaining a foothold.

On the Pike one could also be present at 'The Creation' in one concession, and witness 'The Hereafter', complete with the River Styx, in another. The Boer War was to be seen 'twice daily at 3.30 and 8.30 with an extra matinee on Saturdays and Holidays'. There was even a solar energy exhibit, Harnessing the Sun, an Ostrich Farm and Jim Key – 'The Most Wonderful Horse in the World' – which read, wrote, counted and gave change, and almost stole the whole show. For the more sophisticated the Palais du Costume from the Paris 1900 Exposition or Robbie Burns's Cottage 'containing numerous relics of the Bard of Ayrshire' were available for a suitable entrance fee.

It is small wonder that the Olympic Games, held as part of the exhibition, were overwhelmed, although America won most of the track events. One small item however has survived, at least in America. On the dome of one of the exhibition buildings was a statue entitled *The Victorious Athlete* and small models of this have since appeared at many an American school sports day among the prize trophies.

At the end of the seven month exhibition period, the 1,576 buildings, except those constructed as part of the Washington University campus (part of whose grounds the exhibition had used), were pulled down. As a memorial to the exhibition the Directors presented an equestrian statue of St Louis to the City and, after the books had been balanced, the Jefferson Memorial Building, used today as an historical museum, was erected on the site of the main entrance in what is once more Forest Park. There was one other memento of the hot Missouri summer of 1904 – the ice cream cone which was introduced by one of the concession holders.

Ice cream cones might almost have provided the inspiration for the design of the cupolas of the New Zealand International Exhibition of Arts and Industries held two years later in Christchurch, New Zealand. Very much a colonial event, this exhibition was housed in one main building, a move away from the decentralized approach of the more recent international expositions.

Belgium held international exhibitions at regular intervals after the late 1880s – in Brussels in 1888 and 1897, Antwerp in 1885 and 1894, Liège in 1905, Brussels again in 1910, and in Gand in 1913 when Britain, France, Italy, Holland, Germany and Canada sent exhibits. Although they were more limited in size and attendance, Belgium had held more

93. The Egyptian Quarter: 'A street in Cairo'.
The Antwerp International Exhibition 1894.
(*Illustrated London News* 1894)

shows than France and was truly caught up in the exhibition fever. The 1910 Brussels exhibition, like the Buffalo Pan-American one before it, is mostly remembered because of a disaster. During the afternoon of 14 August 1910 the Grand Palais of the exhibition caught fire and despite all attempts to put it out the building was reduced to a ruin of twisted metal girders by the following day: 'We had spent all day yesterday at the Exposition, which is a very fine one, but returned to Hotel tired out, just an hour before the fire broke out. We went back and watched the fire after tea; it was a splendid sight, but a very sad one'.. (3)

Italy also had two exhibitions, one at Milan in 1906 and another at Turin in 1911. The Milan Exhibition, at which a contemporary chronicler noted that embroidery was most amply represented, even being seen in the decorations of section curtains, banners, and photograph surrounds, was also to suffer the ravages of fire which destroyed the joint Hungarian and Italian art building during the run of the exhibition. The fiftieth anniversary of the re-establishment of the Kingdom of Italy was commemorated by the Turin Exposition which took place within the gardens of the Valentino Castle on the left bank of the River Po. Exhibits were also located on the right bank, stretching for a total of nearly two miles on either side of the River. The banks were connected by a specially built two-level bridge complete with a moving pavement on the lower level. Alternatively visitors could cross the river by either an electrically driven aerial transporter or by more conventional motor launches.

The spate of exhibitions continued with The Lewis and Clark Centennial American Pacific Exhibition in Portland, Oregon, in 1905, the Irish international Exhibition in Dublin in

94. Poster for the Milan International
Exposition of 1906. (Victoria & Albert Museum,
London)

1907 and the Alaska-Yukon Exposition in Seattle in 1909. They were smaller international
events of more local character although the Seattle exposition was interesting in that it
provided the basis of buildings and landscaping for Washington University in whose
grounds it was held. Like London in 1851 it was teetotal, as State Law forbade the sale of
liquor on the University campus.

116

In London in 1908 the Franco–British Exhibition drew the crowds to its ornate plasterwork-decorated pavilions. The Great Stadium, the scene of the 1908 Olympics, was subsequently named White City Stadium after the Chicago-influenced exhibition architecture.

In 1904 Rueben Brooke Hale suggested to the San Francisco Merchants Association, of which he was Chairman, that a great international exhibition should be held in San Francisco to celebrate the completion of the Panama Canal and the opening-up of San Francisco as the 'new trade centre of the Pacific Ocean'. There have been few international exhibitions that have been organized and carried through against such overwhelming odds. The fact that the exhibition was held during one of the most horrific conflicts the civilized world has ever known was but one of the formidable obstacles overcome by the farsighted organizers. Earthquake, fire, war and depression all threatened to crush the exhibition long before it opened. At the end of 1905 it became obvious that certain organizations in Los Angeles were hoping to hold the celebratory exhibition in San Diego and so in January 1906 Rueben Hale, with the help of the Hon. Julius Kahn, San Francisco's representative at the United States Congress, introduced a bill in Washington appropriating the sum of $5,000,000 for an international exhibition in San Francisco. In fact this did not put an end to the San Diego plans, and although it was not so large as its San Francisco counterpart, it provided a second international exhibition in California in 1915.

Only two years after Reuben Hale had proposed the exhibition San Francisco was struck by a terrible earthquake. 28,000 buildings were destroyed by it and the 'Greatest Fire' which followed. Yet six months after these crippling disasters a public conference was held at the Union League Club and the exhibition committee, formed earlier in the autumn of 1906 resolved to form a company 'to inaugurate and hold an International or World's Fair Exposition in the City and County of San Francisco'.

This was at a time when the population was wondering if their fine city would ever be rebuilt and indeed many had already left to set up homes elsewhere. The idea that a major

95. 'Hiram Birdseed starts for the Fair in an automobile'. Portland 1909. (*Hiram Birdseed at the Lewis and Clark Exposition*, 1909)

96. The Court of Honour. Franco-British Exhibition 1908. (*Franco-British Exhibition Illustrated Review 1908*)

117

97. Pilkington's Tile and Pottery Company's
Exhibit. London 1908. (*Franco-British
Exhibition Illustrated Review*, 1908)

international exhibition could be held in San Francisco seemed a pipe dream indeed to the
people who lived through the disasters of 1906.

In January 1907 Senator Edward Wolfe introduced a bill at Sacramento that carried an
appropriation of the sum of $1,000,000 from State funds to pay the expenses of California's
representation at the exposition. This was only supposed to be a beginning and the
Exposition Company intended to match this amount. The Wolfe Bill was passed
unanimously by the Assembly and there were only ten dissenting votes in the Senate.
Unfortunately the State Governor did not recognize the amount of time and money needed
to organize such an event and refused to sign the Bill into law, believing that there was
enough time to proceed with the exposition planning when the State's economy was better
able to carry the cost. On top of this setback, in November 1907, the Knickerbocker Trust
Company of New York was suspended from trading by the New York Stock Exchange.
Money sources suddenly dried up and the United States was plunged into a period of
financial depression. Many large profitable developments had to be cancelled and the
exposition, a project far from being a financially sound investment, was unable to get the
necessary funds to get its plans underway.

Nearly two years of depression followed when the Exhibition Company was only kept
alive by the individual determination and stamina of its Directors.

The action of the President of the San Francisco Chamber of Commerce, James McNab, in
calling a special meeting to ratify the intention of holding an exhibition in San Francisco to

celebrate the opening of the Panama Canal helped to revive the idea publicly, but it was the Portola Festival of October 1909 that finally captured the enthusiasm of the people of San Francisco. Don Gaspa de Portola, the Spanish Governor of the Californias, left San Diego in January 1769 bound for the Bay of Monterey. He sailed past it and in the autumn of 1769 reached the Bay of San Francisco becoming the first white man ever to see it. The carnival held in 1909 to celebrate the rapid rebuilding of the city since 1906, also commemorated de Portola's discovery, and foreign warships were invited to be present in San Francisco Bay during the five days of festivities. The governments which sent warships included the Italian, Dutch, Japanese, German and British whilst Spain and the Netherlands sent their ambassadors. Hundreds of thousands of people danced and sang in the rebuilt streets of San Francisco amidst the confetti, red fire tableaux and myriad electric lights. The celebrations were heralded as a prelude to the planned international event and suddenly the whole exhibition project became vivid, real, compelling and popular.

Four days later the nucleus of the Board of Directors of the renamed Panama-Pacific Exposition Company was formed. They decided to issue a written questionnaire to 2,500 representatives of San Francisco to gauge the city's reactions to the Company's proposals. As Charles Moore, one of the Directors, commented, 'if the public doesn't want the Exposition we shall make a mistake if we try to hold it'. The questionnaire also indicated suitable persons to be called upon by the organizers as the project proceeded. It was a brave and farsighted method of working – such public relations tactics were to be used extensively by the Directors during the organization of the exposition.

Earlier in 1909 Julius Kahn had informed the committee that they would have to find the minimum sum of $5,000,000 in San Francisco to win congressional support and get the necessary national recognition. Following the promise of the first million by forty-two of San Francisco's foremost businessmen, a special subscription meeting was held at the Merchants' Exchange. The second million was promised within minutes of the start of the meeting and by the end of the afternoon the necessary $5,000,000 was assured. But on Kahn's return to Washington it was discovered that New Orleans was also putting in a bid for an international exhibition in 1915 and that Congress was looking for something more in the order of $7,500,000.

The additional money was raised with an issue of bonds by the City of San Francisco and by personal subscriptions from the public. The battle was tough but San Francisco eventually emerged the winner, with New Orleans sportingly admitting defeat and coming out on San Francisco's side. On 15 February 1911 President Taft signed the Act of National Recognition. All that remained to be done was to actually build the exposition. The planning now moved forward at full speed. The problem of finding a suitable site was solved by the decision to build on reclaimed land on the south bank of the Bay of San Francisco, looking out over the beautiful Golden Gate and across to Sausalito. In addition, some private property was purchased by the Exposition Company, and the American Government was persuaded to allow part of its Fort Mason and Reservation lands to be used. The harmonious design of the main exhibition palaces, a break with the scattered architectural effort of many previous exhibitions, was organized by the Architectural Commission headed by George Kelham of San Francisco. Under this a number of specialist groups, including landscape designers, sculptors, illuminators and colorists were also set up. It was the first exhibition to be designed with so much care and thought put into the colour schemes that even the floral planting of the grounds formed part of the overall effect. Jules Guerin of New York designed the colour schemes of the exhibition's main buildings. The colours he used in varying tones were planned both to break away from the fashionable whiteness and to provide the exhibition with gaiety and life. The stark white theme of the Chicago Columbian Exposition architecture that had so dominated American architecture since 1893 was broken. The five colours of pastel pink, ultramarine blue, fawn, burnt-orange and copper green sound harsh and crude when listed but Guerin's careful choice of tone and juxtaposition produced an overall effect of mellowness and warmth. Not since Owen Jones's use of colour in the Crystal Palace nearly sixty-five years before had the colouring of exhibition architecture been so successful:

Your eye is enthralled with the beauty of the coloring. One sees turquoise green domes floating in a silver-moated ether, long colonnades of glacial ice columns leading to regions beyond, where quiet silver pools throw back the mirrored glories. (4)

The main buildings were grouped together at the eastern end of the grounds with the foreign participants to the west of them and beyond that, at the far western end of the site, the sports, aircraft and stock exhibits. The eight main palaces were set out in a distinctive court plan and seemingly formed a single gigantic structure, containing five open courtyards. This colossal group, consisting of the Palaces of Education, Food Products, Agriculture, Liberal Arts, Manufactures, Transportation, Mines, and Varied Industries, was terminated east and west by the Machinery Hall and the Palace of Fine Arts. To the south were the Palace of Horticulture and the Festival Hall. The visitor walking between these buildings was presented with changing vistas out under the decorative arches between them, beyond the Column of Progress, over the yacht harbour and marina to San Francisco Bay and the Golden Gate (not yet spanned by the famous bridge).

Crowning the main building complex at the centre of the southern flank was the Tower of Jewels – a 433 foot high tower built in 'the Italian Renaissance style with Byzantine features' (architecturally the Chicago legacy had not been finally eroded) and covered in 50,000 specially made glass jewels imported from Austria. The jewels in five colours – canary yellow, white, ruby red, emerald green and aquamarine – were each hung from a specially designed hook with small mirrors behind so that their continual motion made the whole tower shimmer with reflected sunlight.

For financial reasons the main structures were built from local timber with a special artificial travertine material made from gypsum, hemp fibre and colouring pigment applied to the exterior to form a glareless wall finish. The exterior of each building was decorated with symbolic friezes designed by Karl Bitter. The sculptures, still very much in the Victorian tradition of mythological representation, were first modelled in New York and then shipped to San Francisco where they were enlarged and multiplied by means of a Pointer, a special three-dimensional pantagraph, in the exhibition's modelling shops under the direction of A. Stirling Calder. The buildings also bore inscriptions selected by Porter Garnett, and a special pocket-size volume was on sale which visitors could carry around with them and which pointed out the symbolism of each and every sculpture, inscription and style of architecture. Even the lighting effects were analysed from a symbolic viewpoint:

This great *Tower of Jewels symbolizes the Panama Canal*, the jewel today that is most resplendent.
The *tower is in seven lifts,* surmounted by the *earth* with its shimmering jewels. You are reminded that the whole earth is affected by this stupendous piece of engineering (the Panama Canal).
Watch, when the Tower is first illuminated with the *Blood Glow*, and you will see that it almost pulsates with life. It should, for is it not the vital part of this great Exposition? (5)

Designed by Walter D'Arcy Ryan, the lighting effects were one of the main attractions. The majority of the light fittings were very carefully concealed within the architectural design, behind sculpture, in hidden lighting troughs and even in the foliage of the landscaping so that they did not detract from the overall design effects during daylight. Great use was made of indirect lighting and reflections from the hidden sources off the faces of the buildings. A battery of searchlights was used, and on special days the Scintillator, which consisted of two banks of forty-eight searchlights, each 36 inches in diameter, produced an hour-long programme with fireworks, smoke bombs and maroons. The clouds of steam, used for the red, blue and green lights to play on, were produced by a motionless railway locomotive carefully painted fawn to resemble the travertine wall of the Palace against which it stood. The display culminated in a gigantic finale which heralded the close of the Exposition for another day.

Although in general it was a serious and intellectual affair, the exposition had a large amusement Zone at its eastern end of which the undoubted star was Stella – a nude painting

98. Official Panama-Pacific International Exposition Poster designed by P. W. Nahl of Berkeley. San Francisco 1915.

99. Souvenir ticket for San Francisco Day at the Panama-Pacific International Exposition showing the Palace of Fine Arts. San Francisco 1915.

of a suitably well-endowed young lady delicately covered in a thin fabric veil in the best Victorian traditions, with the added attraction of an automated breathing bosom – all for a dime! Among the other attractions of the Zone was a five-acre model of the Panama Canal viewed from a moving platform of cars in which visitors sat on two tiers of seats. The total journey through the exhibit took twenty-three minutes and as the spectators passed the various points of interest they could listen to a sound commentary on telephone handsets relayed from a bank of forty-five Edison Phonographs timed to coincide with the visual presentation. This forerunner of our modern audio-visual techniques had been invented and built by Thomas Edison's laboratory and received a Grand Prize under the Liberal Arts section, being the only Zone exhibit to do so.

The main talking point inside the Palaces was the general use made of motion pictures. For the first time the public was able to see films showing the actual use of machines and views of the scenery and people from different lands alongside the static exhibits. Even Siam had a film on her resources and people, and the exhibition itself was to be the first to be advertised in local movie theatres.

Many of the foreign participants had been kept away by the war clouds over Europe but the Avenue of the Nations was still surrounded by the pavilions of twenty-four nations, including France. Although the central government had moved to Bordeaux following the German invasion, Captain Baker, the Director of Exhibits, visited France and persuaded the French Government to participate, before continuing on to Italy. The French had one of the largest foreign pavilions. It was built in the short space of nine weeks, and displayed exhibits that had been brought across the Atlantic and through the Panama Canal by the returning U.S. naval collier *Jason* which had been to Europe to take Christmas gifts to the children of the warring nations. *Jason* also carried the Norwegian, Greek and Italian exhibits, and picked up small consignments from Bristol, Barcelona, Budapest and Vienna. Her arrival at San Francisco on Sunday 11 April 1915 and the unloading of her cargo filled the last empty places in the waiting pavilions. Once again the exhibition organizers had won the battle against almost overwhelming odds.

So impressed were the people of San Francisco with France's fortitude that when they came to consider the possible forms a war memorial might take, they decided to use the plans of the French pavilion. Today the Legion of Honour contains a fine art collection, including many Rodin sculptures, and forms a memorial both to the dead of the 1914–18 war, and the tenacity of France.

100. W. J. Bryan speaking at the celebration of Independence Day. San Francisco 1915. (*The Story of the Exposition*, 1915)

The State pavilions, varying from Oregon's Parthenon (with tree trunk columns) to Pennsylvania's reproduction of Independence Hall, were located next to the foreign buildings. New York State's exhibits included an 11,000lb. cheese, while a river of corn poured forth from a Horn of Plenty in Iowa's building. In the Palace of Transportation, Ford's turned out eighteen cars a day in a special demonstration of the mass-production lines of their Detroit factory, while out on the aviation field the aviators displayed their skills for the crowd. They were not always successful. Lincoln Beachey, who had flown his plane through the Palace of Machinery on New Year's Day 1914, was killed while demonstrating before the crowds on 14 March.

Within the Palace of Fine Arts there was an international exhibition that many considered comprehensive enough to teach the visitors much of the evolution of art. It was the talk of San Francisco – indeed it was estimated that it attracted over ten million visitors. However, critics like Christian Brinton considered that it was merely another example of the increasingly bad methods of display of the arts exhibits at American international exhibitions.

The Palace was designed by Bernard Maybeck, a former tutor of Willis Polk. Polk was Chairman of the original exhibition Architectural Committee set up in 1911 and was responsible for the planning of the Zone amongst other areas, but due to pressure of work he asked his drafting office to come up with some ideas for the Art Pavilion. At that time Maybeck, aged forty-five and down on his luck, was working as one of Polk's draftsmen, and he produced a charcoal sketch which led to his design being accepted and a place on the architectural commission.

No words can describe the great poetic beauty of this Fine Arts Palace. It seems to be the pivotal part of the Exposition, the goal of all pilgrimages, the altar on which you place your ideals. It has so many moods that one must see it in all seasons, during all times of the day, and especially under the illuminations. (6)

Maybeck got the credit for his design but Polk only gave him his draftsman's pay for the project. Today the Palace of Fine Arts can once more be visited. In 1967 it was completely

101. The San Diego Museum of Man. San Diego 1915–16.

102. Night view of the International Exhibition. Rio de Janeiro 1922–23. (*Livro de Ouro Commemorative do Centenàrio de Independência do Brasil*, 1922–23. Instituto Historico e Geografico Brasileiro Collection)

reconstructed, although not in the original colour scheme, at ten times the cost of the first building. The Palace of Horticulture was less lucky. It survived until 1955 but was then pulled down.

The pastel city by the sea will not leave us, for, as the years go on whatever be our mission, the vision of this dream-city will float before us, leading us to finer higher works, strengthening our ideals, and causing us to give only of our finest fibre. (7)

Thus the Victorian idealism of 1851 was echoed by one of the authors of the many guide books and historical reminiscences. But the seeds of change were being sown in Europe, and in many ways international exhibitions would never be quite the same again.

Meanwhile, in San Diego, the much smaller Panama–California Exposition was also being held, setting the precedent of two international events in one country at the same time and even in the same part of that country. During 1915 San Diego was hardly international in scope – in fact it set out to recreate some of the mystery and poetry of the old Spanish days of Central America – but when the Exposition in San Francisco closed many of the foreign exhibitors moved their displays to the San Diego site, which opened for a second year in 1916.

The architecture of the San Diego exhibition was almost completely influenced by the Spanish-Colonial style, reflecting California's historic ties with Spain since the late seventeenth century. Some of the buildings, including the California State building which today houses San Diego's Museum of Man, were intended as permanent structures but the remainder were scheduled to be removed at the end of the exhibition. In the event many remained, and were used twenty years later in a second San Diego exhibition, the California Pacific International Exposition of 1935, which was held on the same site in Balboa Park above the city.

In South America in 1922–23 an international exhibition commemorated the centenary of Brazil's declaration of independence from Portugal's Empire in 1822. Brazil had been one of the most consistent foreign exhibitors at international shows, and fourteen foreign nations participated as well as all the Brazilian States. The Exposição Internacional do Centenario, with its Mexican Baroque architecture, was located in Rio de Janeiro looking out across Guanabara Bay to Niterol, and was visited by over three and a half million visitors including the President of Portugal.

At the same time, almost six thousand miles away in London, Britain was preparing for what was to prove one of the last great shows of her Empire.

CHAPTER NINE
Between the Wars

I declare the British Empire Exhibition open and pray that by the blessing of God it may conduce to the unity and prosperity of all my peoples and to the peace and well-being of the world.

King George V, 23 April 1924 (from BBC recording of the first ever Royal Broadcast)

In 1919 the plans for a British Empire Exhibition, discarded in 1915, were revived. The Exhibition would not only display the countries of the Empire, it would also be a 'Family Party of the British Empire – its first . . . since the Great War, when the whole world opened astonished eyes to see that an Empire with a hundred languages and races had but one soul and mind, and could apparently without any of the mechanism of organization, concentrate . . . all its power for a common purpose'. (1) It would show, in short, that the British Empire was still very much a power to be reckoned with.

A privately organized Festival of Empire had been held in 1911 to celebrate the coronation of King George V. Three-quarter size replicas of the parliament buildings of all the member countries, each one housing its exhibits, had been built in wood and plaster in the grounds of the Crystal Palace's new Sydenham home. It was the biggest event ever held there and it finally bankrupted the Crystal Palace Company – the Palace passed into public ownership in 1913.

All the international exhibitions held in London since 1851 had included exhibits from

103. Leaflet/brochure advertising the British Empire Exhibition of 1924. (Official publication, 1923)

the member countries and colonies of the Empire, but it was not until after the 1911 Exhibition that many people felt that it would be appropriate to hold a nationally organized exhibition of the Empire on a full international scale. These plans had been overtaken by the first world war, but were then resurrected.

The site chosen for this great exhibition of Empire is now a part of suburban London. In 1924 when the exhibition opened its gates it was open parkland, and the visitors from abroad could experience 'all the charm of a gracious bit of English countryside' (2) and on summer evenings could enjoy the 'smell of the new-mown hay'. (3) The site did have other attributes apart from its 'hilly, irregular and finely wooded' (4) environment. Two of London's underground railways passed on either side of it. The Metropolitan Line ran to the new Wembley Park Station opposite the north entrance and the Bakerloo Line had a station at Wembley Central where the London Midland and Scottish Railway also stopped. The London and North Eastern Railway from Marylebone, which stopped at Wembley Hill at the south end of the exhibition, even built a loop and special station actually in the grounds. There were also trams and buses from all over London which ran to the London General Omnibus Company's specially built station which boasted that it could handle up to 200,000 people per hour. The famous pioneering work in poster and graphic design, especially in simple uncluttered typography and artwork, of what is now London Transport, greatly influenced the exhibition's own printed publicity.

The period was an exciting one for advertising and there was an ample supply of creative thought available to produce all the print and presentation design necessary. The British architectural scene, however, was not so alive with inspiration. The old ideas still held sway and as the exhibition looked back at the history of the Empire, it was inevitable that the architecture would reflect the traditional style of the major buildings of the

104. Aerial view of the British Empire Exhibition 1924–25 with the Wembley Stadium opposite the Canadian and Australian Palaces (Aerofilms Photograph)

Empire. The exhibition architects held control and they mostly favoured the neo-classical design, although the recent discovery of Tutankhamen's tomb led to a slight shift in the origins of some of the decorative motifs used. The modern engineering was often hidden, and only the detail and application of modern square finials to pillars and portico, and the addition of Assyrian-inspired motifs altered the façades in any way. Altogether the light-coloured false stone used in construction and the classical architectural styles were very reminiscent of Chicago's exhibition in 1893.

The only buildings that showed any creative thought did so because of either the engineers or the advertising designers. Among these the Palaces of Engineering and Industry, with their reinforced concrete and steel framed roof structures, albeit surrounded by classical colonnaded exteriors, indicated future trends. The main feature of the exhibition, the great Empire Stadium, was a good example of a modern building method without modern building techniques – the 25,000 tons of concrete needed to build it were mixed by hand! The stadium was built in just 300 working days at a cost of £750,000 and was even completed early enough to be used for the 1923 Cup Final. The enormous crowds that came to that Cup Final made Wembley Stadium internationally famous overnight.

The ground on which the Stadium stood might have been the site of an even more unusual monument. At the end of the nineteenth century the Metropolitan Railway Company had purchased Wembley Manor and subsequently sold and leased portions of both the house and the estate to the Metropolitan Tower Construction Company for the purpose of a holiday and recreation area. Sir Edward Watkin, promoter of the idea, decided that Wembley Park should have a suitable symbol on the hill at its southern end and had put in hand the construction of a tower that was to be based on Eiffel's design but which was to be 200 feet higher. Unfortunately public interest was not strong enough and the project had to be abandoned. It remained in its half-built rusting state as Watkin's folly until it was blown up in 1907 and the debris was removed to make way for the Stadium.

During the exhibition, the Stadium housed a wide range of spectacular shows, including a Rodeo put on by the London impresario C. B. Cochran, whose genuine cowgirls caused some comment in the papers. There were also large massed-band concerts and a Pageant which illustrated the growth of the Empire. But perhaps the best remembered events in the Stadium were the firework displays by Messrs James Paine and Son, which included gigantic set-pieces and people in asbestos costumes covered in fireworks to give added movement, and the Navy, Army and Air Force Torchlight Tattoos with their stirring martial music.

Within the pavilions the general standard of exhibition design reflected the architects' neo-classical approach. Fluted columns and pleated fabric valaria contrasted strangely with the modern style of much of the artwork and publicity material. There were some unusual ideas among the exhibits – Dorman Long, the steel suppliers, had commissioned Sir Edwin Lutyens to design their pavilion in the Palace of Engineering. He produced a neo-classical temple with marble-faced columns which was supported by his clients' steel framing. The framing, however, could only be viewed either from an overhead crane, not accessible to the public, or from inside the stand through the small gaps left for the purpose on each column.

In the Palace of Arts were to be found all the latest works of art, among them the tiny and exquisite workmanship of the Queen's Dolls' House, also designed by Sir Edwin Lutyens and containing contributions from all the leading British artists, writers, craftsmen, needlewomen and decorators of the time. Like many of Wembley's buildings, the Palace of Arts still stands, now used for the storage of the props and scenery for the annual ice pantomimes held every year at Wembley's Empire Pool. Another sort of art could be seen at Messrs Pears' Palace of Beauty where living models posed as the most beautiful ladies of history. However, many visitors felt that the exhibits of the various Imperial pavilions were far more interesting than those of the big palaces. Here were to be found the magic of the Far East, the wide open spaces of Africa and the displays of the three great members of the Empire: India, Australia and Canada. In the Canadian pavilion stood an equestrian statue of the Prince of Wales, President of the Exhibition, made entirely of butter – one of the most widely remembered exhibits.

Throughout the exhibition much of the fun was provided by the small kiosks built along the banks of the ornamental lake and inside the large Palaces of Engineering and Industry. Here the advertising designers had been responsible for many weird and wonderful objects, among them stands for Sharp's and Mackintosh's toffees with gigantic reproductions of their tins forming the tops to their booths, stalls for the cigarette manufacturers (Abdulla's was complete with two costumed attendants copied from their trade mark), and the Eno's Fruit Salts Kiosk with its garlands of artificial grapes and the figure of a small boy on top of its domed roof. Many of these stands had been designed by the same man, Joseph Emberton, who had been given an almost completely free hand by the exhibition organizers. His splashes of colour and inventiveness greatly helped to relieve the overall effect of the great plain palaces. Even the Fleetway Press, the official publishers of the guide books and maps, had a specially designed kiosk complete with a Wembley Lion on its central column. Although perhaps a rather obvious symbol for the exhibition, the style of lion chosen was in keeping with the current fashion for things Egyptian. It appeared on all exhibition publicity and in various forms including small china souvenirs. Nevertheless it was not always popular: 'It was Assyrian. It was cowardly (because its tail hung down instead of waving in the breeze), it was unnatural (lions at the Zoo are not like that), it was, in fact, very un-English and, therefore, exceedingly disturbing'. (5) The lion was but one graphic design adopted by the exhibition, which had posters by E. McKnight Kauffer and other famous poster artists, and even a special alphabet designed for the lettering in the Palace of Engineering. This was based on the Trajan's Column Inscription and issued to the exhibitors in the form of a specially produced guide for their signwriters.

Solid cast-concrete lions sat at the great steps up to the main entrance to the building erected by His Majesty's Government. Inside could be found exhibits showing the control and care taken by the mother country over her great Empire. There were illuminated maps showing the location, population and resources of the entire empire, displays of the armed forces, the post office, the tropical health departments and the war they waged against diseases like malaria, the Royal Mint and all the other branches of the Imperial government.

Inside the exhibition grounds were fifteen miles of roadways with names chosen by Rudyard Kipling. Visitors could walk or else ride along them in the Railodock electric buses. There was also the Road-Rail system – its half road–half rail vehicles had two sets of wheels, one to run on the road, the other on rails – and a new development of the Trottoir Roulant of the 1900 Paris Exposition – the Neverstop Railway. Designed by William Yorath Lewis and his assistant B. R. Adkins, this offered a transportation service round the eastern half of the site. The motive force to move the eighty-eight cars, each seating eighteen passengers with a further twelve standing, was provided by a spiral drive system. The cars ran on rubber-tyred wheels and were driven along by this central drive at up to 24mph. They were so spaced out along the spiral that they never touched each other. As its name implied it never actually stopped but merely slowed down at the stations where the pitch of the spiral was altered on the central drive. There were no serious accidents and it was so successful that for the second season of Wembley it ran free of charge. At the south end of the Never Stop Railway was to be found perhaps the most successful part of the entire exhibition: the Amusement Park. Its attractions included a giant switchback railway, scenic railway, dancing hall, a gigantic reproduction of a coal mine which could be visited via a two-deck cage, the tomb of Tutankhamen, and all the more usual sideshows, as well as the famous Water Chute which was to reappear at so many of the future British exhibitions at the White City, Earls Court and elsewhere. The whole exhibition was opened again in 1925 with new amusements and revitalised exhibits and although technically a colonial exhibition the Wembley Empire Exhibition of 1924–25 truly offered a trip 'Round the World for Eighteenpence' as its publicity had suggested.

The 1925 Exposition des Arts Décoratifs Modernes in Paris was to give its name to a whole new international design style, Art Deco. The Exposition had been planned by the

105. Cover of the official Map and Plan with Herrick's Lion. Wembley. 1924–25

French to show the very latest in modern design, and the organizers even went as far as issuing a directive to the exhibitors that the exhibition was to be 'confined to articles of modern aspiration and real originality'. The result was to make most countries exhibit the maximum of novelty with the minimum of traditional influence although the authorities also asked that all the items should meet a practical need. The displays thus showed a certain resemblance – another step down the path to the international uniformity of today.

The exhibition was held on part of the traditional Paris site. Many of the buildings were exceedingly sculptural in form, while bas relief and other three-dimensional decoration,

Opposite
106. The salon of 'Le Pavillon d'un Collectionneur' designed by Jacques Ruhlmann. Paris 1925. (*Arts et Décorations* 1925)

107. Official poster for Exposition Internationale des Arts Décoratifs et Industriels Modernes designed by Robert Bonfils. Paris 1925.

MINISTÈRE DU COMMERCE ET DE L'INDUSTRIE

PARIS·1925

EXPOSITION INTERNATIONALE DES ARTS DÉCORATIFS ET INDUSTRIELS MODERNES AVRIL·OCTOBRE

IMPRIMERIE DE VAUGIRARD·PARIS

108. Bronze commemorative medal for the Paris Exhibition 1925. (*Arts et Décorations* 1925)

131

109. Motor-car decoration by Maurice Dufréne. Paris 1925. (*Arts et Décorations* 1925)

both exterior and interior, were much in evidence. Traditional ideas were definitely unfashionable, and even the Grand Palais of 1900, which was used as one of the exhibition buildings, had its interior completely remodelled. The false ceilings, columns and great open spaces complete with an Escalier Monumental resembled an enormous palace from the ancient world. For, like most modern styles, this one had its roots in the very tradition it was usurping.

As in the 1900 Exposition the pavilions of the great Paris department stores with their careful groupings of designs from many countries, had some of the most interesting exhibits and buildings.

The geometric and unromantic approach of the Art Deco style mirrored the modern science-based world into which western man was driving himself ever more quickly. With its speed shapes, integrated letter forms, rising sun motifs, simplification of form, and general bright colour schemes, its use of the early plastics and all the new metal technology of the aircraft industry, the style was to be prominent in exhibition design right up to the beginning of the Second World War. Even today vestiges of it can still be seen in stretched and crimped crêpe paper and corrugated cardboard window displays of some small shops.

110. The 'Pomone' Pavilion of the Grands Magasins du Bon Marché – contemporary postcard. Paris 1925.

111. The British Pavilion – contemporary postcard. Paris 1925.

132

112. Pavillon de l'Esprit Nouveau designed by Le Corbusier. Paris 1925

If it was the avowed intention of the Paris exhibition organizers to show the very latest in terms of 'modern aspiration and real originality' at Paris in 1925, they certainly did not show it with one of the most sensational exhibits. Le Corbusier had been working for some years on La Ville Contemporaine, and had shown his ideas for a City for Three Million Inhabitants at the Salon d'Automne in 1922. At the 1925 exhibition he displayed plans for the construction of part of such a modern city in Paris, with high rise buildings releasing the surrounding land for use as recreation areas and landscaping. The display of this *Plan Voisin* was housed in a full-size replica of one of the double cube apartments that would be stacked together to form a typical high rise block. Gone forever was the façade of the architectural styles and in their place was a construction which was conceived on the basis of form following function. The Exposition authorities had already given Le Corbusier one of the worst sites for his Pavillon de L'Esprit Nouveau but the crowds found it soon enough and the general reaction was anger that anyone should consider the destruction of their lovely city – especially to replace it with such monstrous buildings. The Exposition authorities, realizing during the construction that they had a piece of real originality on their hands, promptly placed a fence around it so that nobody could see it properly. The result, of course, was to make it even more notorious. Nevertheless the international jury wanted to award Le Corbusier first prize. But the French Academicians used their veto on the grounds that 'it was not architecture', and the only real piece of originality and modern aspiration in a sea of Art Deco styling was carefully and officially ignored, although the 20 foot high fence was removed just before the Exposition opened at the express direction of the French Minister of Fine Arts who personally overruled the opposition of the exhibition authorities.

In the summer of 1925–26 Logan Park, Dunedin, was the site of The New Zealand and South Seas International Exhibition which attracted exhibitors both from the Pacific area

and the British Empire. Like the former Australasian exhibitions which had been organized by Joules Joubert, the Dunedin Exhibition was run by a private company.

In 1926 Philadelphia was again the site of a celebration of the founding of the United States of America. This time it was the 150th anniversary and the Sesqui-Centennial Exposition, almost alone among exhibitions, actually opened a day early although some pavilions were still unfinished. The crowds who flocked through the main entrance with its 25 foot high Heralds of the New Dawn pylons (very reminiscent of the 1925 Paris Exposition's main entrance) to view the pavilions and enjoy the amusements on League Island had to contend with one of the worst summers on record. Almost inevitably it made a loss of just over $200,000. It had been the organizers' intention to build a massive Tower of Light on the 1901 Buffalo pattern but in the event the cost had proved prohibitive and construction stopped halfway, the steel structure being capped by a gigantic searchlight. Instead the crowd had to make do with an 80 foot high, 80 ton reproduction of the Liberty Bell.

The Persian pavilion with its Moorish mosaic façade and gorgeous internal decoration proved a favourite with the crowds, while the great American force of the twenties, thirties and forties, Radio, was ever present through the gigantic horn speakers of WCAU. Notwithstanding the loss, Philadelphia did at least gain a new sports stadium and also the reclamation of a large plot of land that had hitherto been a swampy rubbish dump and an eyesore.

Like the 1924 Empire Exhibition, the proposed Barcelona International Exhibition suffered from the effects of the First World War, albeit indirectly. Spain was not involved in the fighting which broke out during the preliminary building of the exhibition but the project had to be temporarily halted after the war ended when it still seemed impossible to get the necessary foreign exhibitors to agree to the suggested dates. Plans for an exhibition had originated in 1913 when a group of electrical manufacturers conceived the idea of holding an international electrical exhibition. Consideration of the remarkable success of the 1888 Barcelona exhibition however had led to the proposal being altered to provide for both an international electrical exhibition and a general Spanish exhibition. The King, Alphonso XIII accepted the presidency of the enterprise, thus placing the entire exercise under the control of the central Spanish Government.

The post-war indecision of foreign participants which faced the Barcelona organisers led them to suggest a trial run with an International Exhibition of Furniture which they proposed to open on 13 September 1923. But more dramatic events were in store for Spain. This date the beginning of the overthrow of the monarchy which finally ended in a military dictatorship. The new Spanish rulers saw the proposed exhibition as an ideal chance to improve their relations with the rest of the world and accordingly changed the exhibition's scope yet again. It was now to cover Industry, Sport and Spanish Art and was to be held in conjunction with an exhibition the following year at Seville to form a gigantic General Spanish Exhibition. Seville, the scene of the Exposición Ibero-Americana of 1930 contained the exhibits from the foreign countries indicated by its title and was a relatively modest affair. In contrast, the 1929 Barcelona International Exhibition was one of the most spectacular events of the inter-war period. In particular, the lighting, as befitted an exhibition originally suggested by the Spanish electrical industry, was superb. No expense was spared and the great lines of Art Deco style glass lights, leading up to the enormous illuminated fountain with its water cascades just below the main exhibition building on Montjuich, were never to be surpassed.

Opening off the Plaza de España with its massive central Monumento a Colón, two enormous towers framed the rows of lights up each side of the Avenida Reina Maria Christina, with the specially built Palacia Nacional crowning the vista. On either side were the main exhibition pavilions and behind, in what is now a gigantic park, were the foreign and national pavilions and other attractions.

Like Le Corbusier's Pavillon de l'Esprit Nouveau, the German pavilion, which was designed by Mies van der Rohe, indicated the changes that the Bauhaus and its functionalism were to have on both architecture and design over the next decades. The

114. Official advertising sticker for Exposición de Barcelona (Pueblo Espanol), 1929

115. 'Barcelona chair' designed by Mies van der
Rohe for the German pavilion. Barcelona 1929.
(Photo Peter Kibbles)

original idea had been to represent a sequence of modern rooms ending in an open
courtyard, but the pavilion organizers did not know how to furnish it and van der Rohe,
not wanting to see his modern architecture spoiled by traditional styles (as Habitat 67 was
thirty-eight years later), designed the furniture for it. The most famous item was his
Barcelona chair, the exhibition ones being covered in white kid. But it was not only the
chair which had the very best (and most expensive) finish. The walls of the pavilion were
decorated with onyx! It was indeed a very expensive pavilion, well up to the usual
standards of international exhibition displays with their incredibly expensive and
beautifully made exhibits far beyond the average person's pocket!

In 1929 another event of importance to the future of International Exhibitions had
occurred. This was the final agreement of some of the major nations of the world to an
international convention* which would help control both the frequency and the
organization of these massive events, and thus overcome the problems of too many
exhibitions held too often, with the resulting financial and diplomatic problems.

In 1930 Belgium held the International Maritime and Colonial Exhibition as part of the
official centenary celebrations of her independence from Dutch rule. The exposition which
was held in Antwerp, had pavilions from most of the European countries as well as the
seemingly obligatory native village, and could boast architectural styles as diverse as mud
wall, Art Deco and an enormous British pavilion in the style of Wembley and Chicago.

Although the Wembley exhibition had lost nearly £2,000,000 the French, undeterred,
produced a colonial exhibition of their own in 1931. It was not limited to French colonial
exhibits, Italy, Portugal, Holland, Denmark, Belgium and America all exhibited – the last
a reproduction of Mount Vernon, George Washington's house.

* See Appendix I for a detailed description of the evolution of the agreement.

Bruxelles. — Palais du Centenaire
Brussel. — Eeuwfeestpaleis

116. Palais du Centenaire – contemporary postcard. Brussels 1935.

117. Italian Pavilion designed by Libera et de Rengi. Brussels 1935.

118. Official Exhibition symbol – contemporary advertising calendar card. Brussels 1935.

Among the national exhibits the reproductions of the Angkor Wat Temple from what is now Cambodia, and a North African village complete in every detail, were in direct contrast to the Art Deco modernity of the Cité Internationale des Informations complex and the Sections Metropolitaines by the main entrance.

With its slogan 'See the World in a Day' the exhibition more than mirrored the Wembley show, and, thanks to grants from the city of Paris and the French Government, it managed to make a small profit. A permanent result was the establishment of a museum of France's Empire, The African and Oceanic Art Museum, which still stands in the corner of the Bois de Vincennes where the exhibition was held around Lac Daumesnil.

In 1935 Belgium held another international exhibition. The site, in parkland to the north of Brussels, had many mature trees which added to the visual impact of the exhibition, and the central group of buildings remained as a permanent exhibition centre and the home of the Brussels Fair under the title Grand Palais. In 1958 they were used once more as part of an international exhibition. The most popular feature among the exhibits was Old Brussels – an accurate historical reconstruction of past times, which reflected the public love of the old well-known features amongst so much that was new and strange. The Belgian railways commemorated the opening of their first line, between Brussels and Malines, on 5 May 1835, with a display which was also much admired.

Plans for a Chicago exhibition resulted from the suggestions of some prominent citizens that in 1933 the city should commemorate the centenary of its founding, or the centennial of its incorporation as a city four years later. Disagreements caused delays, and the project was cancelled once, but finally members of the public were invited to contribute either $1,000 to become Founder Members, or $50 to be Sustaining Members of the non-profit making body which was to organize the exhibition. They received nothing for their money, not even a free entry ticket – only the satisfaction of knowing they had helped to get the show on the road, and being able to claim their contributions against income tax. Nonetheless, $270,800 was given. When the Fair closed in 1934, it was one of the few exhibitions to have made a profit. The $688,165 was subsequently shared among Chicago's artistic and cultural centres.

Once again the chosen site was along the shore of Lake Michigan although this time it was much nearer downtown Chicago, being on reclaimed land on either side of the site of the present Burnham Park Harbour.

In its early days, the fair was badly struck by the collapse of the American financial system and the depression that followed it. Only the refusal of the Chicago organizers to see the fair cancelled, plus the fact that it provided many badly needed jobs for Chicago's citizens, kept the event going. Even so it was soon apparent that few of the hoped for collective exhibits, to be organized by the various trade associations, were going to materialize because of a lack of money, petty jealousies and an innate sense of competition.

The organizers therefore found themselves with very few national or foreign exhibitors (most countries could no longer afford to participate). Something had to be found to fill the gap, and that something was the National Research Council. Science had affected the last hundred years of American life more than anything else, and the National Research Council was an organization that could provide the whole story of past scientific achievement and present day discoveries, and was only too willing to do so. It was therefore arranged that a series of pavilions should be built to cover the various facets of science and that the fair should become the first international exhibition dedicated to Science. Exhibits were not just to be displayed on plinths – the stories of their invention, design and manufacture were also to be shown, with the help of universities, industries and individuals. The pavilions were designed in the latest Art Deco style. Almost without exception they provided dark windowless space for the exhibition designers to lay out and light just as they wanted without the worry of their effects being spoiled by the sun. The large expanses of exterior blank wall were decorated with bas-relief sculpture and applied decoration, and also provided Joseph Urban, an architect and stage designer who was the colourist to the fair, with plenty of surfaces on which to use his new casein paints. These bright red, orange, yellow, blue and green paints had caused some difficulties. The whole

fair had to be painted in less than three months in inclement weather and the paint finish had to last through the hot summer. There was also the problem of making the strong colours Urban wanted. Such colours had never before been made for use on so many surfaces in such an unsuitable location, with the possibility of sandstorms, rain, insects, and temperatures which could blister paint on metal sidings. In the event the casein paint solved all the problems even making it possible to spray some of the larger areas.

Apart from the brilliant colours the other major problems that the organizers had to contend with were in the Midway area of the fair where the uncontrolled use of loudspeakers and the even more uncontrolled actions of the fan and oriental dancers caused trouble. The most famous of the fan dancers was undoubtedly Sally Rand, who quite happily recounted to the eager newsmen that she had not 'been without work a day since I took my pants off'. There was also talk of Mafia control of much of the Midway although no information could be found to support the rumours.

Among the varied foreign exhibits and displays, the Belgian Village concession proved extremely popular. Other exhibitors obviously took note, for when the fair opened again

119. Pylons, Hall of Social Science at the North end of Electrical Group. Chicago 1933–34. (Chicago Historical Society Collection)

120. The travel and transport building – contemporary postcard. Chicago 1933–34.

Aerial View of
Travel & Transport Bldg.
"A Century of Progress"
Chicago 1933 World's Fair

121. Exhibitor's sticker with the Empire Exhibition symbol. Glasgow 1938.

WE ARE
EXHIBITING
PALACE OF ENGINEERING

EMPIRE
EXHIBITION
SCOTLAND 1938
BELLAHOUSTON PARK GLASGOW

in 1934, eleven other villages opened too, and the visitors were overwhelmed by them all.

From the cars of the overhead *Sky Ride* with its two 628 foot high towers and twelve double-decker rocket cars carrying visitors one third of a mile across the central lagoon, the visitors could look down on the multi-coloured buildings, flowered lawns and the Grand Fountain in the north end of the lagoon. At night the whole scene was transformed into a bright fairyland of coloured lights and the aluminium and glass rocket cars were followed by powerful searchlights as they crossed back and forth with coloured steam coming out behind them. It was as though the world of supermen and rocketships from the comics had come alive.

One of the most unusual buildings at the fair was the Travel and Transport Building which looked rather like a contemporary radio cabinet. For 'the first time in architectural history a dome has been constructed on the principle of a suspension building'. (6) Its designers, Messrs Holabird, Bennett and Burnham, had evolved a method of hanging the dome roof of their building 125 feet above the ground without any central support, allowing the maximum amount of free space for the exhibits below, and finally bringing to completion an idea Bogardus had proposed for the 1853 New York World's Fair.

After 1925, other British Empire exhibitions took place between the two world wars. South Africa held one in 1936 at Johannesburg, and 1938 saw another which took place in Bellahouston Park, Glasgow, where Thomas S. Tait, the chief architect, finally broke away from the traditional choice of classical design for British exhibition buildings.

A year earlier in 1937, Paris was once again the scene of another great French Exposition Universelle. Larger than any previous Paris exhibition, the Exposition Internationale des Arts et des Techniques Appliqués à la Vie Moderne, covered the whole area of the traditional site, as well as finally closing the gap and covering the left and right banks between the Champ de Mars and the Place des Invalides. The Eiffel Tower, decorated with six miles of fluorescent tubes, was once again the central feature – each evening there was a firework display from the first and second stages – but the old Trocadéro Palace which had survived from the 1878 Exposition was pulled down to make way for the new Palais de Chaillot. Designed by the architectural team of Carlu, Boileau and Azéma, the new Palais followed the basic form of the old one with wide sweeping wings enclosing the gardens, but a completely open terrace area between the wings allowed visitors to view the whole magnificent vista over the Iéna bridge and down the Champ de Mars beyond the Eiffel Tower. Below the Palais de Chaillot the fountains from the old Trocadéro were re-designed and enlarged, with huge water jets being added to pump even more river water than before. In addition a new art gallery was constructed – Les Musées d'Art Moderne.

140

122. Souvenir postcard showing the Tower of Empire on the right. Glasgow 1938.

Despite the currency crises and the recent depression, the exposition was designed and carried through in the grand manner. The two most prestigious buildings were those of Germany and Russia which faced each other across the Champ de Mars, reflecting the twin blocks of the Palais de Chaillot and forming strong dramatic elements in front of the Eiffel Tower. The effect was not entirely accidental. Albert Speer, the designer of the German pavilion, tells in his 'Memoirs' the fascinating story of how he 'by chance stumbled into a room containing the secret sketch of the Russian Pavilion', while on an early visit to Paris, and was able to design the German pavilion as a suitable foil to it! They were monuments rather than buildings and both had sculptured symbols at their peaks: 'the gigantic statue of a marching man and woman, sickle and hammer in hand, atop the Soviet building does not miss anything in the effect produced by its location just across from the German pavilion with its great gold German eagle on the highest point of the beautiful, Doric, structure'. (7) The Russian housed the most costly single exhibit in the whole exhibition – a wall map showing the industrial growth of Russia made entirely from gold and semi-precious stones. 'Large rubies in the shape of stars mark the capitals of the provinces and the oil-pipelines from Baku are shown in the form of a long bracelet of topazes'. (8) The rest of the pavilion consisted of propaganda in the form of photographs of 'happy, smiling Communists in field and factory, a tractor or two, a few automobiles and a generous sprinkling of photographs of Stalin and quotations from communist writings'. (9) The main hall of the German pavilion had a magnificent display of the work of contemporary German artists, including work in mosaics, tapestry and stained glass. Elsewhere models, plans and actual exhibits showed the huge increase in Germany's exports since the slump. The whole pavilion was remarked upon for its dignity and lack of overcrowding of exhibits.

The most extensive of the foreign pavilions was the Italian. Inside, displays showed every aspect of life under Mussolini, with a bias towards promoting Italy's tourism.

These three pavilions were also the first finished in an exhibition that was bedevilled by lateness. The official opening date was moved back three weeks in an attempt to get the buildings and exhibits completed but it made little difference. There were civil disturbances in Paris and the unions would not allow extra labour to be hired unless the Government would agree to find other jobs when the exhibition closed. Even the weather did little to help with a cold, wet spring. People wondered if the show was really worth all the strife and worry and many delayed visiting it until they had seen the general reaction. In the event it proved well worth waiting for. Even the most biased visitor was impressed by its size and contents.

123. The Russian and German pavilions facing each other across the Champ de Mars – contemporary postcards. Paris 1937.

The organizers had been at great pains to design their exhibition so that some of the buildings could remain as permanent features – in fact this probably helped to account for the delay in completion. One of these buildings was the Museum of Modern Art. With its two enormous wings joined by a central colonnade, it had to be supported on 1,800 piles driven into the river bank and was a massive project on its own. The new Palais de Chaillot and its fountains had also involved much skilful construction work with many associated problems.

Throughout the Exposition the display and exhibition techniques of both designers and architects reflected the development of a modern style which frequently represented the revitalization of historic design techniques into a modern form. The fountains on the Chaillot Hill were a good example of this: 'The fashionable fountains of eighteenth century France return in full vigour to delight the eye in Celestial Ballets on the Seine where a 4,000 horse power motor helps to pump forty-five times the volume of water in the famous fountains of Versailles'. (10) There were other examples in the use of statuary, bas-reliefs, metal grilles, mosaic and mural painting.

Amongst the national and trade pavilions the large picturesque section devoted to the French Provinces and the halls exhibiting the latest features of modern life were very popular. The official title and objectives of the exposition were to show the latest in art and techniques, and the planners carefully hid the traditional buildings erected by the

Opposite
124. The central courtyard and pool in front of the Museum of Modern Art. Paris 1937.

142

143

125. The Palais de l'Air. Paris 1937.
(*L'Illustration*, 1937)

Provinces and Colonies out on the Allée des Cygnes, in the centre of the River to the south-west of the Eiffel Tower, as well as on the land beside the Tower so that the modern architectural effect should not be spoiled.

Aluminium had first been shown at the 1855 exhibition when it had been classed as a precious metal owing to the difficulty of refining it. At the 1867 Exposition Napoleon had ordered a dinner service made in it. Now in 1937 it had a pavilion to itself. Plastics, although few in number and based on very new technology, also had their own pavilion. Elsewhere visitors could see the speed of development of communications in what one visitor to the exhibition called 'this modern world of fierce international bickerings, this age of gin, jazz and genius, this temporary period of hip flasks and zip fasteners'. (11) There was even a Pavilon de Linoléum, a Palais de la Radio with daily demonstrations of television, a pavilion of cinema, photography and gramophone records and other pavilions on transport, among them a vast imaginative hall for the rapidly developing aero industry and its corrugated metal, piston-engined passenger planes with their basket chairs and feeling of adventurous pioneering. One of the few developments in movie technique, now available in nearly all commercial cinemas, had its first showing at Paris in 1937 on a gigantic 297 foot by 33 foot screen. Making use of the anamorphic lens Henri Chétien's development is better known today as *Cinemascope*.

In contrast to all this was the retrospective exhibition held inside the new Museum of Modern Art. French paintings, tapestries, manuscripts, sculptures, missals, ivories and etchings from the fourteenth to the nineteenth centuries were displayed there, with an exhibition of Van Gogh paintings as an added attraction.

Many people hoped that the exposition could remain open for a further year and for a time even the authorities seemed in favour. But the worsening political situation defeated the idea. Only three years later, Hitler was to pose for the press photographers on the terrace of the Palais de Chaillot with the Tower behind him, having refused to climb up the stairs (the French Army had ordered Etienne Marc, the Tower's director, to wreck both the radio masts and the elevators and lifts when the defeat of Paris seemed assured), and France was suffering another humiliating defeat.

144

CHAPTER TEN
World Fair Competition

You will be astonished and amused and enlightened –
To be abroad at home –
To be on the stage, behind the scenes, and in the audience,
To be in the realm of tomorrow on the rim of today.

New York World's Fair, 'Going to the Fair', 1939. Anon.

The report of the opening day's celebrations of the 1939–40 New York World's Fair shared the front page headlines of *The New York Times* with the latest news of Hitler's ultimatum to Poland. Even the usual plethora of grandiose poetry and prose almost automatically brought forth on such occasions reflected the unhappy and unsettled state of things in comparison to the glorious futuristic world prophesied at the Fair.

The Fair officially celebrated the 150th anniversary of the assembly of the first session of the Federal Congress in New York, and the inauguration of George Washington as first President of America, which had taken place on the balcony of Federal Hall in downtown Wall Street. But New Yorkers were more concerned that the Fair should have a beneficial effect on their future, just as the Century of Progress Exhibition had helped Chicago extricate itself from some of the worst effects of the Depression. Certainly the Fair itself showed that good could come out of bad. Its Corona Dumps site out on the north corner of the Bronx was an area that had long done duty as one of New York's main garbage tips. With its heaps of rubbish and pools of foul water, it was not an immediately obvious site for a prestigious World's Fair. But like their Philadelphia cousins before them, the organizers and particularly New York's energetic Parks Commissioner, Robert Moses, could see its potential and its subsequent future as a great park. It already had $40 million worth of New York Subway on its doorstep, as well as major rail and road links. The exhibition, built on the aptly renamed Flushing Meadow, was certainly a great and successful one but there were pollution problems as a result of the land's former use. The girls who appeared in Billy Rose's famous Aquacade were reported to suffer bleaching of the hair and other unpleasant side effects due to the large amounts of chemicals that had to be added to the water of the man-made lake they performed in!

The theme of the Fair was 'The World of Tomorrow', and its design was centred on two large white structures – the Trylon and Perisphere – which contained an exhibit on the city of tomorrow, Democracity. At the start of the planning Grover Whelan, the Fair's President, had pointed out that if Chicago's Century of Progress in 1933–34 had looked back over the last 100 years, New York was going to 'look forward to a Century in the making'. New York designers and architects who met to draw up the basic exhibition proposals supported this idea and gave it additional substance by publishing *The Fair of the Future – 1939*, a document which set out a proposal urging that 'the Fair should dedicate itself to the future, with the underlying social objective of demonstrating, not mere mechanical progress as in the past, but the ways in which new machines and merchandise could be used to improve economic conditions'. They also recommended that the old method of letting sites to various exhibitors on application with little thought to the proximity of contrasting exhibits, should be discontinued and that the site should be arranged in various co-ordinated sectors. Each sector should consist of a central core exhibit surrounded by the displays of appropriate companies and organizations. (In the event there were seven sectors: Government, Transportation, Communications, Production and Distribution, Food, Community Interests, and Amusements, all except the Government and Amusement sectors having a central exhibit designed and organized by the Fair authorities.)

With such a strong team at the helm, including as it did four architects, one landscape

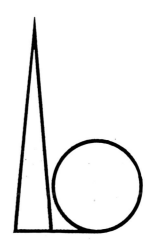

126. The official symbol for the New York World's Fair 1939–40.

127. US Post Office 3 cent stamp commemorating the 1939 New York World's Fair showing the Trylon and Perisphere. (Courtesy US Postal Service)

architect and one industrial designer, many Americans hoped that the Fair would produce some strong architectural style to reflect the country's vitality. They were disappointed. As in 1893, the world's most dynamic country produced an exhibition of singularly dull pedestrian design which in no way rivalled the architecture of Paris's 1937 show or that of the Glasgow Empire Exhibition. A great deal of work had gone into the planning and organization of the exhibition, but breakdowns in the overall scheme began to occur. Many American corporations ignored it – they had after all, paid to be there. The organizers, who had no direct government support, found they had insufficient authority to impose regulations on the exhibitors and could do nothing.

The very nature of the site – 1,216½ acres of flat land traversed by a small sluggish river, which broadened out into a lake at one end – also limited the planning possibilities. The chosen plan of arranging the various sections of the Fair along a series of wide boulevards radiating out from the central feature was admirable in principle, but masses of flags, pylons, booths, and statuary blurred the lines of the buildings and in many cases completely blocked the view down the main vistas. The central Constitution Mall in particular was affected. Whilst the individual components of the Mall were admirably suited to their purpose the sheer number of different features made it almost impossible to gain the effect so successfully exploited in Paris. From the central feature with its 200 foot diameter Perisphere and 700 foot high pointed Trylon painted white, the colouring of the other buildings had been planned in sections. They were to be painted in progressively darker shades of the same colour, from very pale pastel tints near the theme structures to basic rich hues for the buildings on the outside perimeter of the Fair. But once again the overall effect was ruined by the many multicoloured flags and banners down each of the main dividing boulevards and the refusal of some of the exhibitors to conform. Many buildings were decorated with murals ranging in size from small details to massive themes like that for the Food Focal Exhibit depicting food as a source of energy and health. Although they added to the general brightness and gaiety, they too destroyed the attempt at a harmonious colour scheme.

The architects of both the Russian and Italian pavilions had obviously been impressed by the design of the Palais de Chaillot at Paris in 1937 – in fact the Italians actually built a similar cascade of water into their pavilion. Both buildings had central features supported on either side by giant exhibition halls. The central tower of the Russian building carried the figure of a worker who held aloft a star-shaped red light which was visible from most parts of the Fair ground.

Inside, the pavilions suffered from the massing of too much in too large a space. The Russians offered everything from full-size reconstructions of the newly built Moscow Underground stations to a model of the proposed Palace of the Soviets made in precious stones. A contemporary observer summed them up: 'Russia is distinguished by its vulgarity. Italy stands out for its dullness'. (1) Even so, Russia's worker and Italy's goddess Roma were both striking features at night when lighting schemes minimized the effects of the masses of surrounding building.

The Swedish building, probably the best at the Fair, had been designed as a vehicle for the display within it. Its cost had not been high, as the dedicatory stone beside it stated: 'It is with modest resources that our country participates in this contest between the nations of the World'. Finland too had an imaginative display by Alvar Aalto which included a great photographic and timber mural along one wall and 'more original display notions in this one building than in half a dozen others put together'. (2) In fact the building in which it was placed was nowhere near large enough for it all. The largest single exhibit among the national and trade displays was that of the Railroads, reflecting the strong position that they still held in the American economy and way of life, although it was a position they were soon to lose. Here was a massive cavalcade of trains with everything from full-size reconstructions of early steam engines to the latest in high-speed name trains, some even appearing before an audience of 4,000 in a theatrical performance *Railroads on Parade* on 'A stage designed to accommodate two standard gauge railway tracks, highways for vehicular traffic, a performing cast of two hundred, and a channel in the rear for the

128. The interior of the Swedish pavilion. New York 1939–40.

passage of early water-craft. Stage and back-stage occupy five and one-half acres. There are four performances daily'. (3) The same show, known as *Wings of a Century – The Romance of Transportation*, had already been successfully shown at Chicago's Century of Progress Exhibition.

The aeroplane was once again the subject of one of the best pavilions as it had been in Paris in 1937. Designed by William Lescaze and J. Gordon Carr, the grey, blue and white building, containing four full-size aircraft suspended in space from the roof, and its aluminium-covered corrugated asbestos-sheet hangar provided a shape that suggested flight in both fact and form.

The commercial exhibits, particularly those of the major corporations, were far more illustrative of the dynamic American way of life than the official pavilions. Inside, the earnestness of the Chicago exhibits in 1933–34 had given way to a much more lighthearted and popular approach which found expression outside with the National Cash Register Company's gigantic cash register clocking up the daily attendance figures for the fair. The latest and the newest ruled the day. The Depression was hopefully forgotten and the modern American was looking forward to continuing his consumer orientated, mass production, automated life once again.

On the lighter side, the Fair's amusements ranged from *Merrie England* to a Congress of

129. The two ship prows of the Marine Transportation Pavilion façade. New York 1939–40. (*L'Illustration*, 1939)

Beauty and Sun Worshippers' Colony, and included the usual handful of native village reconstructions as well as the Lifesaver Candy Parachute Jump, with a giant steel tower and controlled drop parachutes. Nearby, in one of the few permanent buildings at the Fair, Billy Rose presented his famous *Aquacade* which he had perfected at the Great Lakes Exposition in Cleveland two years before. Based on Hollywood's fabulously successful Busby Berkley routines which had helped to cheer so many people through the Depression, Billy Rose and his Aquabelles in their bright swimming costumes, dived, danced and swam their way through a series of formation routines on the stage and in the pool, with its water-jet stage curtain, to the delight of the capacity crowds.

The New York City Building, which, apart from the railway stations and landscaping, was the only other major feature to remain after the close of the Fair, was to be used again in the 1964–65 Exhibition. In the interim period it provided indoor sports halls and was the first home of the United Nations. Unfortunately the war in Europe too quickly made itself felt at the Fair. Before the close, the flags of the French and Polish exhibits were draped in black, and a notice outside the still uncompleted Czech pavilion apologized for the fact that work had stopped, due to the Nazi invasion. Germany had not participated, but Japan, soon to bring the Americans into the war, did and showed among the other exhibits in her building (almost the only one of traditional design – apart from those of the American States) a model of the Liberty Bell in pearls.

Although the deficit of the Fair was a staggering $18,723,222 it managed to re-establish some of New York's pride, largely destroyed by the catastrophic stock market crashes. Unfortunately this financial loss and the gathering war clouds prevented any work being carried out on the site to produce Robert Moses' Flushing Meadow Park. But at least the Corona Dumps had been tidied up and were somewhat more sanitary.

There had been competition for the New York Fair inside the United States. Across the country San Francisco was once again hosting a World's Fair – The Golden Gate International Exposition. The two great bridges which had been built to link San Francisco with its neighbours across the Bay had recently been opened and to celebrate the event, and at the same time provide the city with a new airport, a great international exposition was held on a specially-built island in the centre of the San Francisco–Oakland Bay Bridge where the needs of both land aircraft and the newly introduced Pan American Trans-Pacific seaplane Clippers could be met. The architecture of the exhibition was specially

148

designed to provide three buildings which could remain after the Fair to serve as hangars and a central control and terminal building for the new airport.

The new bridge had already made use of the existing Yerba Buena Island as a mid-point anchorage, and the shoals to the north provided the ideal base for the specially-built Treasure Island of the 1939–40 Exhibition. But it is doubtful whether this could possibly have been a suitable site for an airport. The prevailing winds which blew in from the Pacific Ocean were so strong and unpleasant that the planners virtually surrounded the site with the solid walls of the exhibition pavilions like a mediaeval walled city, omitting only the side protected by the mass of Yerba Buena Island. They softened the effect of this by planting artichokes, cabbages, palms and other hardy plants around the basically simple forms of their modernistic buildings. The colour scheme by Jess Stanton, the official Chief of Color who was responsible both for the decoration of the buildings and the night time effects of the lighting on them, combined the mellow soothing tones of Guerin's 1915 pallette with the bright strident colour effects of Urban's 1933–34 Chicago.

At night the whole Fair was carefully illuminated and the new coloured flourescent tubes and the even newer ultra-violet 'black light' lamps provided the exhibition vistas with varied and dramatic effects; the architecture and the sculptures provided surfaces that seemed specially designed for the purpose of showing off the expertise of the modern lighting engineer.

The Fair was divided by two great vistas. The first stretched from the Esplanade facing

130. An 'open-faced' car of modern design in the automobile exhibit. San Francisco 1939–40. (*Treasure Island 'The Magic City' 1939–40*)

Yerba Buena Island to the Court of Pacifica, with Ralph Stackpole's 80 foot statue of Pacifica standing in front of a decorative and colourful Persian Prayer Curtain of metal stars and small tubes. The second vista which crossed it, ran from the massive Portals of the Pacific entrance with its twin Elephant Towers, to the Court and Lakes of the Nations and beyond to the American Federal Building. In the centre of these two avenues was the main feature of the Fair – the Tower of the Sun. Octagonal in plan, tapering to a cone at the top, the tower was surmounted by a sculptured Phoenix.

In many ways the Fair's layout resembled the 1915 San Francisco Exposition. The main section was again planned and designed under an Architectural Commission headed by George Kelham (Kelham unfortunately died in 1937 when the detailed design work was about to begin and Arthur Brown Jr took over control). Once again it was a basic mixture of vistas and courts opening out between the main pavilions while the foreign, national and amusement areas were located outside the main exhibition core. Elsewhere too there were signs of the influence of 1915 – there was even a scintillator provided by twenty four searchlights mounted on the north side of Yerba Buena Island.

The competition with New York had stopped many of the foreign nations from participating in the San Francisco Fair and with the exception of France, Italy and Norway, the exhibitors were either nations bordering the Pacific Ocean or from Latin America. Some of the commercial exhibitors and concession holders showed duplicates or close copies of New York attractions. Among these was another gigantic cash register, and such popular entertainments as Sally Rand's *Nude Ranch* and Billy Rose's *Aquacade* in the Gayway amusement area.

The Fair organizers saved themselves some of their problems by banning transport to the site by either foot, regular bus or train. Visitors either went by car (it cost 50 cents to use the bridge and a further 50 cents to get into the Fair) or else parked their cars in downtown San Francisco or Oakland and went by public ferry. At the end of the second year of the Fair when war was imminent, the United States Navy stepped in. The Fair was closed and Treasure Island still remains as a West Coast naval station.

CHAPTER ELEVEN
The Resumption of a Great Tradition

We want to make an assessment, in a concrete form, setting out, at all levels of human activity, the situation in the world of today, we want to aid the peoples to become both keenly and dynamically conscious of their obligation to infuse a FIGURE of HUMANISM into this world . . .

Brussels, 1958, 'The Theme of the Exhibition'

The Great Exhibition of 1851 had organized its exhibits into basic categories either by subject or country of origin. Succeeding international exhibitions had done little to alter this basic approach, other than placing the various categories in separate pavilions rather than one gigantic enclosure. Exhibitions had had official *raisons d'être* and many individual pavilions at succeeding exhibitions contained displays which followed a theme in their presentation. The 1855 Exposition Universelle in Paris had a display entitled *L'Exposition Economique* which exhibited cheap everyday articles of practical use from various countries which the 1867 Paris Exposition developed into a section on the History of Labour, again with exhibits provided by the participating countries. In 1873 Vienna copied the idea and Paris in 1889 had a massive exhibit on the history of human habitation, with full-size reproductions of buildings from neolithic times to the present day. In 1900 Paris had even boasted a whole series of small displays, *les Musées Rétrospectifs*, exhibiting the history of the subject material of each section of the main exhibition halls. However, although many major exhibitions had had themes, none had taken a thematic approach and followed it through to any sort of logical conclusion. The political and technical problems of enforcing such a basic design decision on more than forty foreign and numerous national and private participants had proved too great.

Britain had a different set of problems for its proposed 1851 centennial celebration. By its very nature the Festival was concerned with one subject – Britain. At last it was feasible to think in terms of a more heterogeneous exhibition. Thanks to Herbert Morrison, the Festival possessed a central committee who had the weight of both government authority and, more important, government finance behind them. Further, it was more than lucky in the selection of people to plan the various exhibitions. Under the Chairmanship of Gerald Barry a formidable panel of specialists was formed. Its Assistant Chairman was Cecil Cooke, who had been Director of the Exhibition Division of the Central Office of Information since 1946, and was familiar with the techniques of exhibition and display, and the importance of creative thought and design in such events. With him were designers of the stature of James Gardner and James Holland, architects Misha Black and Ralph Tubbs as well as Hugh Casson, the Festival's Director of Architecture, G. A. Campbell the Festival's Director of Finance and Administration, A.D.Hippisley Coxe and M.Hartland Thomas representing the Council of Industrial Design, and Ian Cox the Festival's Director of Science and Technology. Even Peter Kneebone, their Secretary, was a graphic designer and illustrator. With such a committee it was possible to take major decisions with the minimum of delay – a decided advantage as there were only three years from the date the panel was set up to the opening of the Festival! From the beginning the theme, the construction and the display work were all considered together, and the South Bank Exhibition and other Festival displays around Britain were all to mirror this unity.

The narrative approach, as it was then called, was chosen at an early stage. The actual compiler of the display theme was Ian Cox. His approach was to break the story into three main sections: the land of Britain, the people of Britain, and British discoveries and invention. These were divided again into a number of subsections, each dealing with a separate chapter of the story. They were arranged on the South Bank site using the Hungerford railway bridge over the Thames as the natural dividing line between the two main themes, with the Dome of Discovery, designed by Ralph Tubbs, placed in the centre

131. Abram Games's Festival of Britain symbol. London 1951.

151

132. Aerial view of the South Bank Exhibition. London 1951. (Central Press Photos photograph)

as a symbolic brain. Early on it was decided that the exterior treatments of the buildings should reflect the subjects displayed within. The use of different designs for the buildings, and of a small site – 27½ acres – to contain an exhibition of this scope, led to the development of what the *Architectural Review* was to christen Townscape. The planners were to control circulation around the exhibition, providing an interesting and varied juxtaposition of people to buildings. At last the crowd had become an important part of the architectural concept and not a nuisance to be carefully left out of the official architectural record photographs.

The main difficulty was to ensure that people were sent through the exhibition so that they saw the sections of the story in the correct sequence. The carefully organized routes, as well as the split-levels, had surface treatments of water, cobbles, grass or concrete designed to guide visitors unobtrusively in the correct direction. The routes were all signposted, as well as marked out in the official Guide Book, Catalogue and Map, and most people seemed more than willing to be so directed. Nevertheless, the Guide Book pointed out that 'This is a free country; and any visitors who, from habit or inclination, feel impelled to start with the last chapter of the whole narrative and then zig-zag their way backwards to the first chapter, will be as welcome as anyone else.'

This basic control over the viewing audience gave the exhibition designers major advantages in the organization of their displays.

The theme of the South Bank Exhibition was repeated on a smaller scale on board the Festival Ship *Campania* and other parts of the story were dealt with in smaller shows round the country. This idea of a whole series of events linked together to form a country-wide Festival was another new departure and meant that even the smallest village in the country could involve itself in the celebrations. Although the 1951 Festival of Britain was only national in scope it set the scene for the development of post-war international exhibitions.

Mussolini had intended holding an enormous international exhibition in Rome in 1942 but although the neo-classical buildings were quite far advanced, the plans were overtaken by history and never came to fruition. It was Belgium which held the first international exhibition after the war – the Brussels Universal and International Exhibition of 1958.

Continuing a trend that was begun at the 1933–34 Chicago Exhibition, and which was to be followed by many other exhibitions over the next few years, the Brussels show was concerned mainly with science – with the hand of the professional public relations and advertising man never far from view. America and Russia gave details of their space exploits, and there was the first public demonstration of the nuclear fission that had brought the war in the Pacific to such an instant end. Even the central symbol of the Exhibition was based on a 165 million times magnification of an iron molecule – the 360 foot Atomium which overlooked the whole event. There was a restaurant at the top and a bar halfway up which could be reached either by lift or escalator. Although the whole structure was made of steel, the spheres were clad in aluminium with an outer facing of extremely highly polished aluminium foil. The surfaces were broken down into triangular forms, each of which had a small light in its centre, giving the structure a pattern at night to relieve the overall floodlighting.

The exhibition occupied the 1935 site on the Heysel Plateau, but was enlarged by almost 50% by the addition of the Royal Park of Laeken. It was arranged in three main sections – Belgian, Belgian Colonial and Foreign – with support from a section with exhibits from eight international organizations headed by the United Nations, and an amusement area.

Running down the main avenue of the exhibition from the Place de Belgique, in front of the Grand Palais, to the Benelux Gateway, with the Atomium in the centre, was a series of water pools forming the much talked of Water Ladder. A series of alternating still and swiftly running pools each about one foot above the other gave the impression of the water running up hill, especially at night when they were alternately illuminated. The Grand Palais which survived from the 1935 Exposition is best remembered for its new fascia, with the symbol of the Exposition and the dove of peace in bronze surrounded by a myriad of smaller exhibition symbols which were back-lit with pale blue light at night. To the side of the Grand Entrance Hall was the main theme exhibition, Sciences Internationales, with its display of atoms, molecules, crystals, living cells and all the tools of modern science. Across the way was the Palais International des Beaux-Arts, where an excellent exhibition of fifty years of modern art awaited inspection. The first impression of the visitor to the foreign pavilions in the Royal Park of Laeken was of the splendid landscape in which they stood. The undulating grassland, steep stony ravines and the clumps of beech trees provided an almost perfect setting for the many architectural styles. Guillaume Gillet's French pavilion was the structural tour de force but inside, under the gigantic steel roof with its enormous cantilevered supporting arm (which collapsed during construction), there was a real jumble of levels and exhibits. Other countries had not lost sight of the fact that it was an exhibition and some, like Brazil which had a captive red balloon to fill its central roof opening, even had some fun with their display. Britain had a small, beautifully

133. The official symbol for the 1958 Brussels World Exhibition.

153

134. The interior of the American pavilion around its central pool with a mannequin parade underway. Brussels 1958.

designed pavilion but the main part of its site was given over to an industrial display after the style of the British Industries Fairs. This met with a lot of criticism of its confusion of stands and its blatant commercialism. Nevertheless one item met with universal approval – Whitbread's pub, *The Britannia*, which certainly repaid the operators a hundredfold!

In contrast to the Russian pavilion with its mass of technical and industrial exhibits, America showed very little except some modern art, satirical murals by Saul Steinberg, a working drug-store, and other features and comments on the American way of life. This

was all supported by gigantic photographs and a regular mannequin show on the floating
stage in the middle of the pool under the central open roof. Its freedom and
lightheartedness provided a welcome relief from many of the other displays.

Among the other pavilions, simple structures with curtain walls of glass, timber and
faced panels on metal structural frames, some with tensioned membrane roofs reminiscent
of the 1933 Chicago Travel and Transport Building, were in strange contrast to the gilded
temple of Siam and the traditional plaster-coated structures of the Vatican's building – the

135. The interior of the Russian pavilion
arranged around a gigantic statue of Lenin.
Brussels 1958.

155

136. Some of the foreign pavilions (from the left to the right) Canada, USSR, USA, Vatican and, on the opposite side of the Passerelle, the French pavilion. Brussels 1958.

first time the Holy See had participated in an international exhibition. The layout of the exhibition, particularly in the relationship of one pavilion to another, left much to be desired: the Canadian pavilion, for instance, was almost cut off by the great blank wall of the Russian cinema; the French pavilion seemed to only just squeeze into its space next to the Passerelle pedestrian bridge which traversed the dip in the land between the Park of Laeken and the rest of the site, while Liechtenstein found itself in an acreage of open ground.

The Belgian section contained the exhibits of various government departments and some of the private industrial pavilions of the multi-national corporations which have become such a feature of many of the recent international exhibitions. One of these was the Philips pavilion. Designed by Le Corbusier, this was made of reinforced concrete with 300 loudspeakers built into its freely curving hyperbolic-parabaloid structure and presented a

137. Philips Pavilion designed by Le Corbusier. It was made from 2,000 slabs of prestressed concrete, each a different shape, suspended between steel cables. Brussels 1958.

139. The aluminium gothic arches in the central courtyard of the American Science Pavilion. Seattle 1962.

poème électronique with sound, lights and projection playing on the inside surfaces – 'a synthesis unlimited in its possibilities for colour, imagery, music, words and rhythm' (1). It was to be a herald of the forthcoming flood of environmental experiences of future exhibitions. There were also early examples of the multiscreen film and slide techniques that were to almost swamp international exhibitions in the years ahead. The most prominent was the Walt Disney *Circarama* which followed Grimoin-Sanson's 1900 presentation *Cinéorama* in form, and was held in the special circular theatre behind the main pavilion.

Another smaller exhibition dedicated to science was held in America four years later. The original intention had been to celebrate the 50th anniversary of the Alaska–Yukon–Pacific Exposition of 1909 but it was finally held in 1962, after seemingly inevitable delays. The site was small – only 74 acres – by any standards, but the proposers of the scheme had been so struck with the scope of the Festival of Britain which had been held on an even smaller site, that they decided they would rather produce a jewel-box fair near downtown Seattle than go to a larger out-of-town site that would not be so useful afterwards. In addition they realized that the civic buildings already on site could be used. Today, the whole site is still in use as the Seattle Centre, forming a nucleus of artistic, amusement and exhibition and conference facilities for the city.

Once the date and site of the exhibition had been chosen, the organizers, already worried about the potential costs, had to find the finance for it. When they discovered that American scientists, disturbed by the lack of American scientific achievements shown at Brussels, wanted to hold a scientific exhibition but had no site for it, they managed to amalgamate the two ideas – Seattle would hold an international exhibition of the sciences. With the support of the organizers, the scientists presented a definitive and strong case to Congress for financial support. The type of display envisaged, with demonstrations and carefully designed exhibits to explain even the most complicated discoveries and techniques to the public, was to cost far more than Congress originally agreed but the organizers refused to give up hope and finally managed to get most of what they wanted. Invitations to foreign nations were sent out via President Eisenhower just before the vital bill was passed.

The Fair nearly fell at the next hurdle when the plans for the site were presented. They involved massive development and covered far more land than was originally agreed. As one of the Committee reported at the time, 'I fear that you are leading the community by the hand down the road to bankruptcy.' (2) He could have been right – the scheme costed out at $32,000,000 more than the budget!

However once this was sorted out, and the other problems were resolved the organizing committee had to try to get official Bureau International des Expositions approval for their small exhibition. They were in direct competition with the much larger New York event scheduled for 1964. Contrary to expectations, by careful manoeuvering Seattle did win BIE approval and so was able to invite the countries who were signatories to the convention, while because of the time clause in the BIE agreement, New York could not invite any of them. In the event forty-nine countries participated, among them France, which had the distinction of having both the largest display and the only one which gave any hint that science alone might not answer all man's problems. A few of the performers in the Gayway felt the same: 'I'm here to save the Fair from science' (3) declared one of the delectable young ladies in the Exposition's amusement area.

The features of the Exposition that were to appear in most of the publicity, and even on the official postage stamp, were the 600 foot high steel Space Needle, and the Monorail, which carried people from the centre of downtown Seattle to the heart of the Exposition.

The Space Needle had its origins in the Television tower at Stuttgart where Eddie Carlson, the first President of the Century 21 Exposition, had been struck by the fact that people were 'not only here but they paid to get up here. They actually paid a fee to buy a dinner.' (4) It was to become the best known feature of the whole Exposition and appeared on countless souvenirs many of which were produced in Japan which seemed to have cornered the 1962 souvenir market. There was an official trade mark identifying the

138. The official symbol for the 'Century 21' World's Fair. Seattle 1962.

158

159

140. US Post Office 4 cent stamp commemorating the 1962 Seattle World's Fair showing the Space Needle and Monorail. (Courtesy US Postal Service)

Exposition but the Needle soon took over as the Exposition's symbol.

The Monorail had originally been intended as the main feature of the Exposition. It was designed by Alweg of Sweden and built in West Germany in special lightweight alloys. It's two articulated four-coach trains were capable of 70mph, but on the short run in from downtown Seattle they had no chance of reaching this speed. Although dwarfed by the Space Needle, with its revolving restaurant and fabulous view out over Puget Sound and the mountains beyond, the Monorail aroused much interest abroad. As it was free from noise and pollution problems many people saw it as a possible means of urban transport in the near future.

The United States Science Pavilion, covering nearly 7 acres with its six buildings, courtyard and pools, contained an exciting and imaginative exhibit on science and its effects on man with the accent on audience participation. Designed by Minoru Yamasaki, a Seattle-born architect, the group of stunning buildings with their five tall, slender, aluminium gothic arches contained displays designed by Raymond Loewy, George Nelson and Charles Eames. In the entrance hall, visitors were greeted by *House of Science*, a six screen twelve minute film which traced the story of science up to the present day as an introduction to the exhibits. In the centre of the pavilion another film presentation, using the domed roof of the building, gave visitors the chance to participate in a trip out to the edges of the solar system and back.

Elsewhere the State of Washington display in the Coliseum building repeated an idea from the New York 1939–40 Exposition. 'The World of Tomorrow' was once again the subject, but this time it was a walk-through exhibit using 3,700 interlocking cubes as plinths, screens and walls to provide the display. It was reached via a trip on a clear plexiglas-domed hydraulic lift that carried visitors up into the clusters of silver cubes in the ceiling of the Coliseum while the Bubblelator operator intoned: 'Utopia Century 21 – first floor, threats and thresholds, frustrations and fulfilments, challenges and opportunities' like a department store lift-boy.

Many world fairs, including the San Francisco and New York ones of 1939–40, had shown an operating profit which had then been decimated by the cost of both construction and demolition. Seattle had planned ahead, and was to spend only two months clearing away the temporary buildings and fittings to reveal a ready-made civic, cultural and amusement centre with Coliseum, sports arenas, Opera House and Art Gallery as well as exhibition and conference buildings. Like the 1909 Exposition, Century 21 left the city a legacy of outstanding facilities as well as a financial profit.

CHAPTER TWELVE
Madison Avenue and the Computer

There is no doubt that consumers desire this Fair to be a smashing, glittering success.

Sarah Welles, 'Printers' Ink Magazine', 1964.

Seattle was an undoubted success, but the much larger New York World's Fair of 1964–65 probably did more to discredit international exhibitions than any event before or since. Although the theme was 'Peace Through Understanding', there were more arguments and more people upset, from foreign governments to local grocery chain bosses, than would have been thought possible. Cheap tawdry commercialism was finally given its head with predictably disastrous results.

141. One of a series of cartoons of the sights of the 1964–65 New York World's Fair by Ronald Searle for *Holiday* magazine. (Ronald Searle)

142. The official graphic symbol of the 1964–65 New York World's Fair.

The Fair began badly. The organizers applied to the Bureau International des Expositions in Paris for recognition, but described how they planned to alter the Bureau's regulations to fit their own requirements. Then when Seattle's Fair was recognized instead, New York suddenly found itself without any major foreign exhibitors, for they had mostly accepted the invitations to participate in Century 21. Undismayed, Robert Moses, the Fair's chief, directed his energies to filling the empty places with the exhibits of industrial and commercial firms who were keen to use the Fair as a public relations and advertising platform.

Before the second world war there had been a gradual increase in pavilions for individual companies; now suddenly there was an almost overwhelming number, each vying with the others for publicity, originality and popularity. The wheel had come full circle and the showmanship of the mediaeval salesmen had arrived back having spent some years banished to the trade and funfair arenas. This was not to say that some of the results were not well designed and well intentioned; rather that it was extremely difficult to get away from commercialism at the New York World's Fair.

Once again the Flushing Meadow site was used with basically the same layout as in 1939–40. The foundations of the old Perisphere provided a base for the 120 foot diameter Unisphere centrepiece supplied by the United States Steel Corporation, which like everything else, also acted as an advertisement, although the worst excesses had been reduced before the plans were agreed. The gigantic globe with its three encircling satellite paths was 'Dedicated to man's aspirations toward Peace through mutual understanding and symbolizing his achievements in an expanding universe'. (1)

Among the many industrial pavilions the automobile manufacturers, as in 1939–40, proved most popular with the crowds. General Motors had a new Futurama display showing the ideas of their designers. In contrast, Ford's turned to Walt Disney and his audio-anamatronics world of life-like automatons to present a history of mankind. Pepsi Cola, General Electric, and the State of Illinois also had Disney displays with three-dimensional, brightly coloured fairy-tale characters and scenes telling stories to the visitors.

The ovoid building on stilts erected by International Business Machines and designed for them by Eero Saarinen, contained one of the most interesting and innovatory exhibition displays. A gigantic seventeen screen cinema made use of film, slides and live presentation in a programme showing how computers process information in much the same way as the human brain. The audience were lifted 60 feet on the 'People Wall' into the auditorium to see the show. Designed and produced by Charles and Ray Eames, the display below

143. A commercial pavilion based on the trade mark of the exhibitor the Travelers Insurance Companies' red umbrella. New York 1964–65.

featured mechanical puppets and games which provided information for the visitors.

But it was the film shown by the Johnson Wax Company which was one of the hits of the exhibition. The three screen film *To Be Alive*, had been produced by Francis Thompson and Alexander Hammid, and there were no interruptions from the sponsors for commercials – a welcome break at New York in 1964–65! It went on to win the 1966 Oscar as best documentary.

One of the most interesting building constructions at the Fair, and one of the few unifying factors, was the series of Brass Rail Snack Bars with glass fibre balloon roofs designed by Victor Lundy. Unfortunately Lundy's high standards were not matched by the food and service available inside – the *New Yorker* was quick to point out that all seemed 'mysteriously designed for complete chaos and discomfort'.

The disharmony was repeated outside. Throughout the run of the Fair free background music from the Radio Corporation of America clashed with individual pavilion sound-

144. IBM Pavilion designed by Eero Saarinen, one of the last projects he worked on before his death. New York 1964–65.

145. The Electric Utility Companies Tower of Light pavilion built up from 600 aluminium prisms and containing a musical presentation on the benefits of electricity. New York 1964–65.

tracks, and the thousands of makeshift signs vied with the few official ones to create a cacophony both audio and visual.

Although there were no sex shows comparable with those of previous American exhibitions, there were other extravagant entertainments. Many of these managed to lose their shirts, including Mike Todd Jr's *America be Seated*, a $3,500,000 water spectacle à la Billy Rose, and the Texas pavilion's *To Broadway with Love*.

164

The standard of building and the bad site planning which appeared to be based only on financial return, led to much adverse comment and resulted early on in the Fair's planning team resigning.

The Fair opened on 22 April to cold grey skies and rain as well as threats by the Congress of Racial Equality who saw it as a chance to gain some publicity by causing a massive stall-in with upwards of 2,000 cars blocking the roads out to the Fair and demonstrators jamming the rail and subway links, to say nothing of pickets at the Fair itself. In the event they failed to materialize in any great numbers and apart from drowning President Johnson's opening speech and causing a few scuffles the only real effect was to frighten away many of the expected first-day crowds.

Despite the brash commercialism and almost continuous run of bad press reports, Robert Moses remained optimistic and unrepentant 'Some people hate like Hell to see the Fair moving to success', and it struggled on through 1965. Many enjoyable hours were doubtless spent there although it failed to make financial ends meet and returned only 62.4 cents in the dollar to its bondholders.

Unfortunately Moses's dream of Flushing Meadow Park did not materialize and the partly landscaped Park still bears the scars of the Fair – the remains of the US Federal pavilion, the State of Washington pavilion and the old 1939–40 New York pavilion, as well as some statuary and the Unisphere, all liberally scrawled with graffiti. Dereliction is rampant.

The effects of the unfavourable press reports and financial loss of the New York Fair on the organizers of Canada's Expo 67 can be imagined! Luckily the Swiss Exhibition in Lausanne in 1964 did a little to offset the New York disaster. The first Swiss National Exhibition had been held in Berne in 1857 and subsequently at regular twenty-five year intervals in one or other of the major Swiss cities. Designed and presented in the immaculate Swiss manner, with great attention to detail, the 1964 Exhibition greatly

146. Magazine cover by Roy Lichtenstein reflecting the three dimensional Pop-Art architecture of the 1964–65 New York World's Fair. (*Art in America*, April 1964)

influenced the Expo 67 organizers. A monorail and the use of tent-like roofing structures in particular, as well as beautifully integrated graphics, were to do much to encourage the Canadians after the seemingly insurmountable problems in New York.

In 1958 Marc Drouin, a Canadian Senator, had been sent to represent his country at the official 'Canada Day' festivities at the Brussels Exposition. There he conceived the idea of following the American example and holding a great international exhibition as the main celebration of Canada's centennial. He even suggested that his city of Montreal, with its cosmopolitan atmosphere and past experience in the organization of trade exhibitions, should be the location.

Even the Government's Exhibition Commission doubted the wisdom of holding such an event – the reaction of its Director was 'Technically possible, but hardly worth the effort'. However, many Montreal businessmen, formerly sceptical, were surprisingly enthusiastic about the idea, and were strongly supported by Jean Drapeau, Montreal's new Mayor. Drapeau was to remain Expo's most loyal and ardent supporter over the next few years, and was to be instrumental in the choice of Montreal for the 1976 Olympics.

And so the decision was made, and Montreal chosen as the site. As early as 1895 A. S. Brodeur had published drawings showing the islands in the middle of the St Lawrence River opposite downtown Montreal as a suitable location for an international exhibition. The local press supported the idea – 'One of this City's great newspapers proposes St Helen's Island as the site' (2) but attempts to use the islands for expositions in 1917 and 1942 were each interrupted by war. The third opportunity was not to be missed. The 1967 Fair can be regarded as marking the watershed between the more conservative Canadian outlook of the years after the second world war and the lively attitudes of the present. The sixties saw an awakening of national pride, and the adoption of a new flag and new national anthem. Canadian society experienced new tensions and strains with the re-emergence of the Anglo-French problem which was given additional prominence by De Gaulle's 'Vive Quebec Libre' speech, and the subsequent Front de libération québecois crimes. The new national feeling and the increased social awareness, combined with numbers of skilled and creative young Canadian designers, architects and planners, produced an exhibition which will quite possibly remain the high point of the modern international exhibition movement.

Indeed it was amazingly difficult to find fault with Expo 67, although attempts were made, particularly during the planning stage. Inevitably there were some problems – shadflies, the ice on the St Lawrence River – but there was always a feeling that it would be one of the best, a feeling that was obviously international as BIE members argued for the honour of seconding Montreal's application for recognition!

Unlike the New York World's Fair, the Montreal organizers had neither competition to find foreign participants, nor grave financial problems. Money was provided by the City, the Province and the Federal Government, and this financial security and the use of a computer with its Critical Path Method of project control, made it possible for the organizers to plan the Fair around a theme and what is more, carry it out.

The chosen theme of 'Man And His World' was based on the philosophy of Antoine de Saint-Exupéry who developed it in his internationally acclaimed book *Terre des Hommes*. The authorities then created a series of sub-themes each of which was illustrated by exhibits provided by the participating nations in its special pavilion. The basic divisions were:

Man the Explorer: Man and Life; Man, His Planet and Space; Man and the Oceans; Man and the Polar Regions; Man and his Health.
Man the Producer: Resources for Man, Progress, Man in Control.
Man the Creator: Fine Arts; Photography; Contemporary Sculpture; Industrial Design.
Man in the Community.
Man the Provider: Agriculture.

Most of the foreign and national exhibitors also organized their displays around the central theme.

Two additional displays were organized as part of the theme presentation. The first of these, under the direction of the world famous National Film Board of Canada, told the essential story of man. In the specially-designed Labyrinth building with three separate chambers the audience was 'grouped around a series of tiered balconies . . . watching a short film on two 38 × 20ft screens, like Cinerama turned on end. One screen was set into the floor of the building and the other rose at right angles at one end. From the beginning the viewer's eye was disorientated and from that point it never really had a chance. He was used like the ball in a tennis match as the action switched from screen to screen . . .' (3)

The second related display was Habitat 67, an experimental housing scheme designed by Moshe Safdie who was only twenty-four. The concept was simple – house units built

147. The major theme of the 'Man in the Community' section, Moshe Safdie's Habitat 67, with another section of Expo 67 beyond. Montreal 1967. (Architectural Press Ltd. Sir James Richards)

167

one on top of the other so that the roof of one house formed the garden of the next – but the construction and fabrication caused headaches for both the Exposition organizers and the contractors. The individual houses, each with bathroom, kitchen and services installed in the form of factory-finished units, were to be built on a production assembly line. They would then be lifted into position by a giant crane, and be almost instantly ready for the decorators and inhabitants. The problems arose both because of the cost of making the production line tools and moulds and also because, although the finished structure was safe, the gradual building-up caused it to be often out of balance – as anyone who has ever built a similar structure in toy bricks will realize! The original cost estimate was $40,000,000 and the sceptics considered the whole thing a joke when it was first put forward to the Federal Canadian Government (which was far from renowned for its wild spending of government funds) – after all Safdie was an architect who had never built anything before! Surprisingly, the Canadian Government agreed, although it cut the size of the project to one-sixth of the original, and fixed a ceiling of $11,500,000. It actually cost $22,000,000, mostly because the very form of construction entailed just as much equipment and expertise for the 158 housing units as would have been needed for the much larger original concept. Unfortunately the interiors of the houses, with few exceptions, completely failed to reflect the revolutionary thinking of the architecture. Many were designed under the auspices of Canadian popular women's magazines who filled them with some of the worst examples of North American interior design.

The contrast between good exterior and poor interior design was also found in some foreign exhibition halls. The confused German display was housed in a much admired pavilion with a roof structure made from steel net, lined with a translucent plastic skin and supported on eight steel masts. The French pavilion was filled to overflowing with exhibits

148. Buckminster Fuller's geodesic dome American pavilion at Expo 67, with a monorail train about to pass through, viewed from the Cosmos Walk bridge. Montreal 1967.

like a gigantic warehouse, with some fun sculptures sitting on top like the proverbial gilt on the gingerbread.

The architectural, or more accurately, computer-assisted engineering masterpiece of the show was the American pavilion with its 250 foot diameter transparent geodesic dome designed by R. Buckminster Fuller: 'from the inside there will be uninterrupted visual contact with the exterior world. The sun and moon will shine in the landscape, and the sky will be completely visible, but the unpleasant effects of climate, heat, dust, bugs, glare, etc., will be modulated by the skin to provide a Garden of Eden interior.' (4) (Fuller saw this controlled environment as a possible method of extending into the less pleasant areas of the world or even, in time, to completely hostile surroundings like the moon.) The display designers realized, like their predecessors in Brussels, that they could not compete with the structure and settled for displays which worked with the building rather than against it. They did, however, have problems that the Americans had last had at New York in 1853–54. Rain leaked through the dome. The patent silvered-plastic sun blinds, fitted in eighteen segments to each of the 600 window sections and controlled by solar activated motors, also managed to jam with alarming regularity. The effect, especially from the outside, was really very decorative – like lots of flowers in varying stages of opening – but presumably Buckminster Fuller was not amused!

The American, and the Province of Ontario pavilion with its carefully integrated display under another reinforced vinyl tent structure, were the only ones to make full use of the Exposition's Monorail trains by actually allowing them to run through their exhibitions – a unique opportunity missed by all the other participants.

The advanced *Diapolyecran* audio-visual presentation and well-balanced displays of the Czech exhibits caught the public imagination as their pavilion had done at Brussels. The *Diapolyecran* was a particularly exciting development of standard slide presentation techniques. Shown on a 32 × 20ft screen made up of 112 2-ft cubes which glided backwards and forwards, it presented *The Creation of the World* using stereophonic sound effects and more than 15,000 slides. Among the more unusual foreign pavilions were those of Cuba, with its strong ideological graphics, and Ethiopia with a giant tent based on one of the ceremonial umbrellas from the ancient city of Axum. The traditional buildings of Thailand, Burma, Iran and China also added a great deal to the scene.

Many of the smaller countries which had not been able to afford to participate in the recent Expositions exhibited in buildings supplied by the Canadian organizers, and grouped together to form Africa Place and the Arab Nation Pavilions. Some national pavilions included a few surprises – not least the forthright display of the Indians of Canada, with its honest statement of the oppression and problems of being an Indian in modern Canada.

The visitor to Expo 67 could also find something seldom seen at international exhibitions – humour. The British pavilion, for example, had a splendidly original section on *Britain Today*, designed by James Gardner complete with lighthearted references to English habits and characteristics. Multi-media exhibit design was found in many of the pavilions, and was particularly prominent in those of the Canadian Provinces – the Western Provinces even made effective use of smell in its central open courtyard with a gigantic fully-loaded logging truck surrounded by lofty Douglas Pines apparently bringing the smell of the forest into the exhibition.

La Ronde, the amusement section, was bright with coloured banners and sculptures. Among its more unusual features was a marina for people visiting Expo by boat and, as a permanent feature, a gigantic Aquarium, which like many other features, was sponsored by a private company. There was also the Garden of the Stars, an auditorium for a massive programme of world class theatrical events and concerts. The main ride, in a collection of some of the best in the world, was the specially-built triodetic structured *Gyrotron* which offered a trip into space and ended with a confrontation with a mechanical monster rising from a sea of molten lava. It was designed by Sean Kenny, the multi-media stage designer, but its huge structural cost, like that of Habitat, resulted in a lack of money for the interior details so a lot of spectacular ideas never came to fruition.

169

Unlike the New York World's Fair organizers, the Expo 67 authorities had carefully designed both their street furniture and their site signs. They even produced an official manual to show how the signs, designed by Paul Arthur Associates, were to be produced and used.

Apart from Habitat 67 there was no major structural feature at Expo, so that maximum use was made of the Expo 67 symbol, designed by Julien Hébert. It was the first time that a graphic device so successfully supplanted an architectural or engineering symbol and it appeared everywhere – on publicity, flags, ashtrays and other souvenirs – and always under the most careful licensing and design controls.

Just as the American Centennial Exposition in Philadelphia in 1876 had resulted in a massive awakening of national pride, especially in the arts, so the extravagant international success of Expo 67 produced a similar reaction in Canada.

149. The official Expo 67 graphic symbol designed by Julian Hébert. Montreal 1967.

150. The United States Rubber Corporation's development of the ferris wheel. New York 1964–65.

170

A smaller exhibition, HemisFair 68, took place in San Antonio, Texas in 1968. It was recognized by the BIE and had as its theme 'The Confluence of Civilizations in the Americas'. The symbolic tower, The Tower of the Americas, was specially designed in reinforced concrete by O'Neil Ford and reached 622 feet into the sky with the by-now obligatory restaurant at the top. Perhaps the most exciting exhibit, however, was the third of the Thompson/Hammid team's film presentations at international exhibitions. Their film *We Are Young* had used a six screen set-up at Expo 67 to show 'what a frenetic, complex, confusing, eager thing it is to be young at this moment of time'. In 1968 in the United States Federal Pavilion, Confluence USA, dramatized America's rich cultural heritage. There were three auditoriums, each capable of holding up to 400 spectators. The screen on which they each watched the first section of the film expanded for the second part and then, 'as a small plane, relic of early flight, sails into the clouds, suddenly the screen and theatre walls disappear into the ceiling. The three small theatres become a single huge 'confluence' theatre, and each visitor is one of a combined audience of 1,200 which views the third and final phase of the film projected on the world's largest curvilinear screen 38×140ft. Pictures flood the giant screen, engulfing the audience in sights and sounds'. (5)

Japan was the scene of the next great BIE Category One international exhibition. She had applied early for the 1970 date and had sent representatives to both New York and Montreal to watch and record the do's and don'ts of organizing such a large event. Unfortunately this research into other people's experiences stifled originality at Osaka in 1970. It seemed almost as if the organizers had been so careful not to make the mistakes of New York and Montreal that they had little time for innovation. Modern architectural trends, with the emphasis on building materials such as concrete, glass and steel, with little if any applied colour or decoration, seemed to reflect the organizers' concern not to upset anyone with bright colour schemes. However, many commercial exhibitors and even a few of the foreign pavilions, managed to provide the necessary colour, usually in the form of the currently popular bright primary hues. Their displays also showed as much ingenuity as at previous exhibitions, but there was little to compare with Expo 67's theme pavilions. The Japanese central theme of 'Harmony for Mankind' was only slightly dealt with in the interior and vicinity of the gigantic Sun Symbol sculpture at the centre of the massive theme structure. This structure was undeniably spectacular and the thematic exhibits artistically exciting, but they were not as effective as Expo 67 in communicating their message.

The huge central theme area which was designed by Kenzo Tange, straddled the main entrance gate with its specially built bus and subway stations below. It contained a number of focal points, including the Expo headquarters with the Communications Tower and International Bazaar to the south, and the enormous Festival Plaza with its Tower of the Sun, Expo Hall and Museum of Fine Arts to the north.

The enormous transparent roof of the Festival Plaza, resting on six gigantic pillar supports, covered an area of 340,000 square feet and weighed 6,000 tons and had been gently jacked up into position to a finished height of 98 feet. A massive engineering feat, it unfortunately cut the saucer-shaped Expo 70 site in half and although very impressive from a distance it lacked human scale when seen from the site, and from some angles it

151. An architectural section through Kenzo Tange's Festival Plaza showing (from left to right) the Main Entrance Gate Plaza; the Sun Plaza with the Tower of Motherhood and the Central Tower of the Sun with the arena of the Festival Plaza to the right. Osaka 1970. (*Official Report – Drawings of Facilities of the Expo 70 Site*)

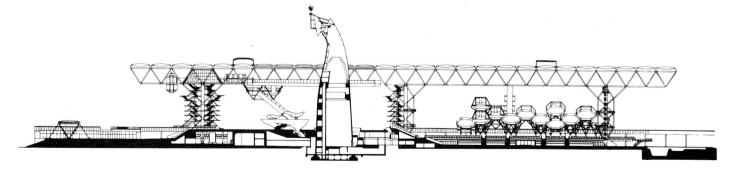

seemed to form an impenetrable barrier. Inside the Festival Plaza area a series of movable units made it possible to create arrangements for everything from a full arena event to an intimate theatre production.

The oriental flavour of this first Asian international exhibition was unquestionably one of its great attractions to the foreign visitor and the sight of parties of Japanese tourists, each with a tour leader with a small telescopic identification flag and the loose crocodile of tourists following in their paper identification hats, gave the whole event added colour.

There was a very high number of foreign participants and many of the smaller nations again exhibited in pavilions provided by the organizers. Among the larger exhibits, the Swiss Light Tree with its 32,000 illuminated spheres was much admired. Russia maintained her traditional approach of a massive building filled with innumerable exhibits, although there were signs that she was beginning to learn from the display techniques of the other nations.

The United States again introduced a revolutionary building design. Their pavilion was not really so much a building as a hole in the ground roofed over with a stretched fabric tent. There had been misgivings in Washington that it would prove an unsuitable exhibition structure because there was virtually no elevation outside at all beyond a slight hump in the ground and a mound of earth. The earth that was dug out was placed around

Opposite
152. The British Columbia pavilion with the low roof of the American pavilion in the distance. Osaka 1970.

153. The language problems of international exhibitions have led to an increased use of pictograms for site signs. These examples from Expo 75 include an unusual one warning visitors of poisonous snakes. Okinawa 1975.

173

154. The view from the West Gate of Expo 70 showing the Fuji Group Pavilion. Osaka 1970.

155. Aerial view of Expo 75 site showing the Aquapolis and the sandy Pacific beaches. Okinawa 1975.

the circumference of the resulting 274 × 465ft. elliptical bowl and a concrete ring was cast on top of it. Steel cables were then laid in a diagonal formation with a vinyl-coated glass-fibre fabric stretched over the top. Raised internal air pressure gave additional support to the centre of the roof. The design of the display inside harmonized with the unusual structure, and even made use of the internal sloping walls of the outer banking.

Some of the industrial exhibitors also used air pressure to help support their buildings. The Fuji group's pavilion had sixteen vinylon inflated tubes, each 13 feet in diameter and 263 feet long, joined together to form a structure reminiscent of an American covered wagon, and over ten stories high. Inside its huge yellow and white walls was a display showing a *Message to the 21st Century* in the form of a total experience using light, sound, projection and movement. In fact it was almost impossible to get away from total experiences at Expo 70. A more conventionally designed exhibition was almost a relief from the mind-blowing attacks of many of the displays, especially those in the Japanese private pavilions. The over-use of audio-visual techniques, including the new projection tube colour television, made it only too easy to overlook good presentations like the one in The Netherlands pavilion where the entire structure of the building had been dictated by the requirements of the walk-through film and slide show.

The Scandinavian countries, exhibiting together as often, also offered a most unusual large, open, barn-like pavilion with projectors throwing pictures on to angled screens supported from the ceiling and, more unexpectedly, on to the floor of the pavilion. As the visitors entered they were each handed a piece of white card with the flags of the five participating Scandinavian countries on it and discovered, much to their surprise, that by holding it in the right place and using it as a screen, they could read the messages projected down from the ceiling of the pavilion. The result was a pavilion full of people finding out about the story of pollution control in Scandinavia in an atmosphere of surprise, delight and enjoyment. The message was clear, the technique beautifully simple, the involvement immense.

Since Japan's Expo 70 there have been two smaller exhibitions in Spokane, United States, in 1974 and in Okinawa, Japan, in 1975. The theme of the former was 'Celebrating Tomorrow's Fresh, New Environment', and for six months it exhibited the problems and solutions to today's polluted environment on two islands in the centre of the Columbia River. The Japanese exhibition, designed around the theme of 'The Sea We Would Like to See', was held in the sub-tropical islands of Okinawa. Here, amidst the sandy Pacific beaches the nations came together once more for another peaceful meeting.

156. US Post Office stamp for Expo 74 with its theme of 'Celebrating Tomorrow's Fresh New Environment'. Spokane 1974. (Courtesy US Postal Service)

CHAPTER THIRTEEN
The Great and the Greatest?

The grandest and most cheerful, the brightest and most splendid show that eyes had ever looked on since the creation of the world.

William Makepeace Thackeray, 1851

This book has only been able to touch on the major international exhibitions held since 1851. There have been many hundreds of smaller exhibitions, and others that were planned but never took place. Often money was not available or a lack of any real interest outside the small band of keen organizers caused the cancellation of grand plans. Sometimes the event has taken place but without the hoped-for foreign participants and sometimes other international events, like war, have intervened.

Had some of the grand schemes materialized, they could have easily ranked with the major exhibitions of the past. On the occasion of the 100th anniversary of the Treaty of Peace and the recognition of American Independence in 1883, New York attempted to hold an International Exhibition on a 300 acre site in the City. The organizers received Washington's approval, and planned to build more than eight Crystal Palace-like structures to house the event. But they failed, as did a second attempt in 1892 – financial problems and local indifference were just too great.

The best known recent failure is probably the Bicentennial Exposition planned for Philadelphia in 1976. Local disagreement over the best site, the poor financial climate and ultimately President Nixon put paid to the idea. Earlier failures include the Rome World Exposition of 1942, which Mussolini had planned to celebrate the twentieth anniversary of Fascist rule in Italy, but which ended with the death of Mussolini and the defeat of the regime it was to have feted. Tokyo's 1940 World Exposition was cancelled because of the second world war. The organizers of Expo 70 in Osaka thirty years later honoured the tickets that had already been sold to the earlier Exposition and had not been redeemed at the time of its cancellation.

Every succeeding exhibition has advertised itself as the greatest event ever held; even the smaller fairs have tried to find something they could claim as bigger, better or more original. Over the years architects, designers, planners and visionaries have suggested various schemes to support such claims. Many of these have failed to materialize, some have re-appeared later in different form while others have just been lost and appear only in obscure publications of the times as examples of creativity, innovation and sometimes sheer absurdity – for example the Bogardus design for the New York Exhibition of 1853–54 or the gigantic theme and feature buildings put forward for the Chicago World's Columbian Exposition of 1893. Other grandiose ideas have included plans to turn the Eiffel Tower into a new and even greater feature at the Paris Exposition in 1900, and to build the Paris/Montreal tower which was to rise 325 metres into the sky on the eastern tip of Expo 67 to represent the 325 years of Montreal's existence. Although these schemes were never built and many have sounded impossible, many of the ideas which did materialize looked just as impracticable at planning stage.

What of the future? Two international exhibitions are planned, one in Los Angeles in 1981 and one in Australia, on the occasion of her bicentennial in 1988. Elsewhere a number of smaller exhibitions are to be organised, but no other major event. The reasons are not hard to find. The western nations which have sponsored most of the great exhibitions are short of money, costs have escalated out of all proportion, and there is the present fear of urban terrorists, as well as union problems. Yet there are other countries which could afford it, and in the past far greater problems have been overcome. In fact attempts were made recently even in Britain to get a Festival underway for the 1980s.

157. The original BIE symbol chosen in 1929.

158. The new BIE symbol designed by a Japanese student in 1969.

Why should anyone ever want to hold another? When one looks at the financial results of these exhibitions it is all too easy to forget the advantages to local businessmen who supply the accommodation, food, travel arrangements, and construction teams. Fairs have made gigantic losses but have added immeasurably to the confidence, wealth and growth of the area in which they were held.

Of course there can be bad effects such as the derelict, rotting wastelands left when there has been no proper control after the event. Expo 70 is a particularly bad example of this, although a plan does exist for a magnificent memorial park and even for a cycle of international exhibitions on the site at thirty year intervals. Other events have been planned well and cities like Seattle and San Antonio have found themselves with civic facilities they may never otherwise have had. While they have provided employment, for instance in Chicago in 1933–34, they can also cause a slump in employment after the event, when hundreds of extra workmen find themselves with skills no longer wanted – a phenomenon which caused at least part of the union troubles of the Montreal Olympics in 1976.

But the factor that finally tips the scale in favour of holding international exhibitions is trade. In the past the host countries have either been industrialized themselves or have formed part of an empire with an industrial base, and just as increased international trade was the ulterior motive in 1851, so it almost always is today.

It is clear that future exhibition must have more to offer the visitor than the majority of the attempts since Expo 67. The organizers of the Paris Exposition in 1925 had the right idea – it is 'modern inspiration and real originality' which are essential for success today, just as they were in 1851.

Appendixes

Appendix One
The Evolution of the International Conventions and the Bureau International des Expositions

The Bureau International des Expositions, with its offices in the Avenue Victor Hugo, Paris, was established after many meetings held between the nations of the world from the beginning of the international exhibition movement. Its date of inception in 1931, eighty years after the Great Exhibition, gives some idea of the problems and diplomacy involved in getting even a basic pattern of control adopted – in fact America has only recently joined the list of official signatories.

The first internationally agreed document appears to be the unofficial memorandum drawn up and signed by Henry Cole and five of the other foreign Commissioners to the Paris Exposition of 1867. They decided that the scope and duration of these gigantic events should be controlled, that they should be held in rotation in various capitals and that although covering the same subjects, they should arrange their exhibits by class rather than nationality with far more careful selection and consideration of the quality of the items. This would result in no increase in the size of future exhibitions.

But it was not until 1912 that a formal diplomatic meeting took place and the International Convention of Berlin was signed by fifteen countries. Unfortunately the first world war effectively ended the agreement. Nothing further was done until 1928 when thirty-one countries met in Paris and produced the 'Convention Regarding International Exhibitions', which is the basis of present agreements. Subsequent amendments have been made and today a proposal to increase the time span between international exhibitions is awaiting ratification. If it is agreed, the intervals between international exhibitions will be as follows:

Kind of exhibition	Organized in the same country	Organized in different countries
Two Universal Exhibitions	20 years	10 years (can be shortened to 7 years by special BIE permission)
Universal and Special Exhibitions	5 years	———
Two Special Exhibitions of the same kind	10 years (can be shortened to undetermined interval)	5 years (can be shortened to undetermined interval)
Two Special Exhibitions of a different kind	5 years (can be shortened to undetermined interval)	2 years (can be shortened to undetermined interval)

As of January 1976 there were thirty-eight signatories to the BIE convention.

The author would like to thank the BIE for their kind help in compiling this section of the book, and their Director M. R. Chalon for his personal encouragement.

Appendix Two
International Exhibition Check List

The following list is not complete. The discrepancies to be found in the records of such events makes a final definitive listing all but impossible. However, the list is based on a considerable amount of research around the world and can certainly be taken as the most accurate one available to facilitate comparison between the various international exhibitions of the past. It has been compiled on the basis of foreign representation (usually a minimum of four official foreign exhibitors) and the method of organization. Because of this, certain exhibitions, like the 1951 Festival of Britain, do not appear on this list although they are referred to in the text. If there has been major doubt about any of the statistics they have been omitted rather than give a false impression. To allow for easier comparison the finances of the exhibitions have been converted to pounds sterling at rates current at the date of each Exposition – it must however be kept in mind that the purchasing power of the pound alters – for example, the 1938 pound sterling was worth about 37p in 1957, and a 1960 pound sterling was worth 69p in 1970. Since most of the exhibitions have been partly or wholly financed by central or local government, if the original grants are subtracted from the results, far more exhibitions made a loss.

Some colonial exhibitions (notably 1886 London, 1924–25 Wembley and 1931 Paris) have also been included, for although they were officially national events they were supported by a considerable number of what are now separate states and in area, volume and importance can rank with many of the other international exhibitions.

The author would be most grateful for any further substantiated information which could help in improving the accuracy of this listing. (International exhibitions which over the years have been recognized as the major events are printed in bold type.)

date	place	title	total attendance	profit/ loss	site acreage	months open	notes
1851	**London England**	**Great Exhibition of the Works of Industry of all Nations**	**6,039,195**	**£186,437 profit**	**26**	**4.8**	
1853	Dublin Ireland	Great Industrial Exhibition	1,156,232	£19,999 loss*	6½ Building only	5.5	*loss met by W. Dargan
1853–54	New York USA	World's Fair of the Works of Industry of all Nations	1,250,000	$340,000 (£70,103) loss*	13	15.5	*loss born by stockholders (private company)
1855	Paris France	Exposition Universelle	5,162,330	Fr8,300,000 (£332,000) loss*	34	6.7	*excludes cost of Palais de l'Industrie
1862	**London England**	**International Exhibition of 1862**	**6,211,103**	**£11,783 loss***	**24¾**	**5.7**	*£11,000 met by J. Kelk – £783 loss
1865	Dublin Ireland	International Exhibition of Arts and Manufactures	932,662	£10,074 profit*		5.3	*cost partly met by B. L. Guinness
1867	**Paris France**	**Exposition Universelle**	**6,805,969**	**Fr2,880,000 (£115,200) profit***	**165 plus 50 annex**	**7.2**	*distributed amongst guarantors, City and State
1871	London England	First Annual International Exhibition	1,142,151	(£30,000 profit in 1871)	12	5	
1872	London England	Second Annual International Exhibition	647,190	see 1874	6	5.5	
1873	London England	Third Annual International Exhibition	500,033	see 1874	6	7	
1873	**Vienna Austria**	**Weltausstellung 1873 Wien**	**7,254,637**	**Fr69,000,000 (£2,760,000) loss**	**42**	**6.2**	
1874	London England	Fourth Annual International Exhibition		£150,000 loss on 1871–4 series	6	7	
1875	Santiago Chile	Exposición Internacional de 1875					
1876	**Philadelphia USA**	**Centennial Exposition**	**9,910,966**	**$5,166,276 (£1,065,211) loss**	**284.5**	**5.3**	
1877	Cape Town South Africa	South African International Exhibition			⅓* Building only	3	*in Goede Hoop Gardens which were also used
1878	**Paris France**	**Exposition Universelle**	**16,032,725**	**Fr31,794,890 (£1,271,795) loss**	**192**	**6.5**	

date	place	title	total attendance	profit/loss	site acreage	months open	notes
1879–80	Sydney Australia	Sydney International Exhibition	1,117,536	£103,615 loss	15 Building only	7	
1880–81	Melbourne Australia	International Exhibition	1,330,297	£1,571 profit	63	7	
1883	Amsterdam Netherlands	Internationale Koloniale en Uitvoerhandel Tentoonstelling Te Amsterdam			62	6	
1883	Boston USA	The American Exhibition of the Products, Arts and Manufactures of Foreign Nations	300,000	*	3 Building only	4	* building constructed by Massachusetts Charitable Mechanics Association as permanent exhibition hall at cost of over $500,000
1883–84	Calcutta India	International Exhibition	(over 1 million)	R$1,390 (£96) loss*	10	3	* after payment of £3,000 to M. Joubert
1884–85	New Orleans USA	World's Industrial and Cotton Centennial Exhibition	3,525,000	final 1886 $250,000 (£51,547) loss*	76	5.5	* exhibition purchased privately for $175,000 in 1885
1885	Antwerp Belgium	Exposition Universelle d'Anvers	3,500,000		54	6	
1886	London England	Colonial and Indian Exhibition	5,550,745	£34,643 profit*	13	6.1	*profit used to set up Imperial Institute, London
1887	Adelaide Australia	Jubilee International Exhibition	789,672	£100 profit*		7	* as at March 1889
1888	Barcelona Spain	Exposición Universal de Barcelona	1,227,000 (paid only)		111	6	
1888	Brussels Belgium	Grand Concours International des Sciences et de l'Industrie			220	6	
1888	Glasgow Scotland	International Exhibition	5,748,379	£40,000 profit	16 Building only	5.4	
1888–89	Melbourne Australia	Centennial International Exhibition	2,003,593	£237,785 loss	22 Building only	6	
1889	**Paris France**	Exposition Universelle	32,350,297	Fr8,000,000 (£320,000) profit	237	5.7	

date	place	title	total attendance	profit/ loss	site acreage	months open	notes
1891	Kingston Jamaica	International Exhibition	304,354		12*	2.7	*excluding Race Course
1891–92	Launceston Australia	Tasmania International Exhibition	262,059	£180 profit			
1893	Kimberley South Africa	South Africa and International Exhibition	339,950	£14,000 loss	3		
1893	**Chicago USA**	**World's Columbian Exposition**	**27,529,400**	**$807,000 (£166,392) profit**	**685***	**6.1**	* including 85 acres Midway Plaisance
1894	San Francisco USA	California Midwinter International Exposition	1,315,022*	$32,464 (£6,694) profit	160†	6.2	* excluding 119,059 visitors before and after † excluding park
1894	Antwerp Belgium	Exposition Internationale d'Anvers	3,000,000		148¼	6	
1894–95	Hobart Australia	Tasmania International Exhibition	290,000		13*	6	* covered area only
1897	Guatemala City Guatemala	Exposición Centro-Americana				8*	* official 4 month run extended for late foreign exhibits
1897	Brisbane Australia	Queensland International Exhibition	220,814*			2.8	* probable loss – exact figures unobtainable
1897	Brussels Belgium	Exposition Internationale	6,000,000				
1900	**Paris France**	**Exposition Universelle**	**48,130,300**	**Fr82,000 (£3,280) loss**	**267***		*plus 276 annex
1901	Buffalo USA	Pan-American Exposition	8,120,048	$578,000 (£119,175) loss	350	6.1	
1901	Glasgow Scotland	Glasgow International Exhibition	11,559,649	£30,571 profit	100	6	
1902	Turin Italy	Esposizione Internazionale d'Arte Decorativa Moderna				7.5	
1902–03	Tonkin (Hanoi) Indo-China	Exposition Français et Internationale				3	* cost Fr5,718,857 (£228,754)
1904	**St Louis USA**	**Louisiana Purchase Exposition**	**19,694,855**	**$19,974,291 (£4,161,310) loss**	**1,272**	**6.1**	

date	place	title	total attendance	profit/ loss	site acreage	months open	notes
1905	Liège Belgium	Exposition Universelle	6,143,157	Fr75,117 (£3,005) loss*	173		*Fine Arts Building and 3 bridges over River Meuse left to City
1906	Milan Italy	Exposizione Internazionale	5,500,000		250	6	
1906–07	Christchurch New Zealand	New Zealand International Exhibition of Arts and Industries	1,967,632	£81,430 loss	14 Buildings only	5.5	
1907	Dublin Ireland	Irish International Exhibition of 1907	2,751,113	£100,089 loss	52	6	
1907	Hampton Roads USA	Jamestown Ter Centennial Exhibition	2,850,735	$2,450,330 (£510,485) loss		7	
1909	Seattle USA	Alaska-Yukon Pacific Exposition	3,740,561	$63,676 (£13,266) profit*	250	6	*excluding buildings for Washington University
1910	Brussels Belgium	Exposition Universelle et Internationale	13,000,000	£10,000 loss	220	7	
1911	Turin Italy	Esposizione Internazionale d'Industria e de Laboro	4,012,776		247	4.5	
1913	Ghent Belgium	Exposition Universelle et Industrielle	11,000,000		309	7.5	
1915	**San Francisco USA**	**Panama-Pacific Exposition**	**18,876,438**	**$2,401,931 (£500,402) profit***	**635**	**9.6**	***Auditorium built for $1,089,780 from profits**
1915–16	San Diego USA	Panama-California (International*) Exposition	3,800,000	**	194†	12‡	*added second year **profit given to San Diego museum †within 1,400 acres Balboa Park ‡open 2 seasons
1922–23	Rio de Janeiro Brazil	Exposiçao Internacional do Centenario do Rio de Janeiro	3,626,402		$61\frac{3}{4}$	12*	*continuously open
1924–25	Wembley England	British Empire Exhibition	27,102,498	£2,000,000 loss	216	12*	* open 2 seasons

date	place	title	total attendance	profit/loss	site acreage	months open	notes
1925	Paris France	Exposition Internationale des Arts Décoratifs et Industriels Modernes	5,852,783		57	6	
1924–26	Dunedin New Zealand	New Zealand and South Seas International Exhibition	3,200,498	£16,217 loss	65	5.5	
1926	Philadelphia USA	Sesqui-Centennial Exposition	6,408,289	$206,987 (£43,122) loss	275	6	
1929	Barcelona Spain	Exposición Internacional de Barcelona			291½	6	Jointly called L'Exposición General d' España
1930	Seville Spain	Exposición Ibero Americana					
1930	Antwerp Belgium	Exposition International, Colonial, Maritime et d'Art Flammand		Fr7,000,000 (£100,000) loss	170½	6	joint Belgium International exhibitions celebrating the centenary of Belgian independence
1930	Liège Belgium	Exposition International de la Grande Industrie, Science, et Application Art Wallon		Fr15,000,000 (£2,142,857) profit*	165	6	* returned to shareholders of the exhibition
1931	Paris France	Exposition Coloniale Internationale	33,500,000	Fr29,000 (£414) profit*	500	6	* excluding African & Oceanic Art Museum.
1933–34	Chicago USA	A Century of Progress International Exposition	48,769,227	$688,165 (£141,597) profit	424	12*	* open two seasons
1935	Brussels Belgium	Exposition Universelle et Internationale de Bruxelles	20,000,000	Fr45,000,000 (£6,428,572) profit	309	6	
1936	Johannesburg South Africa	British Empire Exhibition	1,500,000	£70,000 loss	100	4	
1937	**Paris France**	**Exposition Internationale des Arts et Techniques dans la Vie Moderne**	**34,000,000**	**Fr13,000,000 (£178,000) loss**	**250**	**6**	
1938	Glasgow Scotland	British Empire Exhibition	2,593,232		175	6	
1939–40	**New York USA**	**New York World's Fair**	**44,932,978**	**$18,723,222 (£4,680,850) loss**	**1,216½**	**12***	*** open two seasons**

date	place	title	total attendance	profit/loss	site acreage	months open	notes
1939–40	San Francisco USA	Golden Gate International Exposition	17,041,999	$559,423 (£139,855) loss	400	12*	*open two seasons
1958	**Brussels Belgium**	**Exposition Universelle et Internationale de Bruxelles (Expo '58)**	**41,454,412**		**500**	**6**	
1962	Seattle USA	Century 21 Exposition	9,609,969		74	6	run by private company for one year now run by city
1964–65	New York USA	New York World's Fair	51,607,307	$17,500,000 (£7,000,000) loss	646	12*	*open 2 seasons
1967	**Montreal Canada**	**Universal and International Exhibition (Expo '67)**	**50,860,801**	**$Cdn. 73,218,325 (£24,406,108) loss***	**1,000**	**6**	*as of November 1969
1968	San Antonio USA	HemisFair '68			92	6	
1970	**Osaka Japan**	**Japan World Exposition (Expo '70)**	**64,218,770**	**¥ 19,439,402,017 (£22,600,00) profit**		**6**	
1974	Spokane USA	Expo '74 World's Fair			100	6	
1975	Okinawa Japan	International Ocean Exposition (Expo '75)	3,500,000	¥430,000,000 (£500,000) profit*	250	6	*preliminary estimate

Bibliographic Note and Bibliography

The quantity of books, pamphlets, catalogues and ephemera on any one of the international exhibitions of the past is immense. This note is therefore only intended as a springboard for those wishing to pursue the subject further.

The best places for a researcher to begin are the Royal Society of Arts in London (the author's collection is also available through the RSA); the Bibliothéque Nationale in Paris; The New York Public Library and the Centre for Research Libraries near Chicago. City and university libraries in places where exhibitions were held are also worth investigating.

The researcher should always remember that much of the material was produced in advance and sometimes promised events and constructions failed to materialize! All facts need careful checking as myths grow up over the years – the most famous of these is probably the story that Dom Pedro, the Brazilian Emperor, listened to Bell's telephone at the 1876 Centennial Exposition and dropped it screaming 'My God! It talks!' – sadly there is no evidence for this, and no mention of it can be found until many years after the Exposition had ended!

The following short bibliography only gives reference works which relate to the major international exhibitions and is far from complete. (Publication is in the city in which the exhibition took place unless otherwise noted.)

1851 – LONDON   The Great Exhibition of the Works of Industry of All Nations
The Official Illustrated Catalogue (4 vols) 1851
Tallis's History and Description of the Crystal Palace (3 vols) 1852
Dickinson's Comprehensive Pictures of the Great Exhibition (2 vols) 1854
Gibbs-Smith, C. H. *The Great Exhibition of 1851 : A Commemorative Album* H.M.S.O. 1950
Hobhouse, C. *1851 and the Crystal Palace*, Harvill Press 1950

1855 – PARIS   Exposition Universelle
The Official Report: *Rapport sur l'Exposition Universelle de 1855*, 1857

1862 – LONDON   International Exhibition of 1862
The Official Catalogue: *Illustrated Catalogue of the International Exhibition*, 1862 (this contains a very good survey of earlier exhibitions in Volume I by J. Hollinshead) (4 vols)
The Illustrated Record of the International Exhibition of the Industrial Arts and Manufactures, and the Fine Arts of all Nations, in 1862 1863 (also contains material on 1851)
The International Exhibition of 1862, H.M.S.O., 1962

1867 – PARIS   Exposition Universelle
The Official Report: *Rapport de la Commission Impérial. Précis des opérations et liste des collaborateurs avec un appendice sur l'avenir des expositions*, 1869
L'Exposition Universelle de 1867 Illustrée, (2 vols) 1867
Horne, A. *The Fall of Paris – The Siege and the Commune 1870–71*, London 1965 (the first chapter, 'The Greatest Show on Earth,' captures the period flavour of the exposition probably better than any other recent English writing)

1873 – VIENNA, Weltausftellung 1873 Wien
Reports on the Universal Exhibition of 1873 (4 vols) London 1875
L'Esposizione Universale di Vienna del 1873 – Illustrada Milan 1873 (also published in France and Austria)

1876 – PHILADELPHIA   Centennial Exposition
The Official Report: *U.S. Centennial Commission: International Exhibition 1876; Report of the Director General* (2 vols plus Appendices) 1879
The Masterpieces of the Centennial International Exhibition, (3 vols) 1876
Treasures of Art, Industry and Manufacture represented in the American Centennial Exhibition at Philadelphia 1876 1877 (a folio of colour lithographs)
Maas, J. *The Glorious Enterprise – The Centennial Exhibition of 1876 and H. J. Schwarzmann, Architect-in-Chief*, American Life Foundation, New York 1973

1878 – PARIS   Exposition Universelle
The Official Report: *Rapport Administratif – Exposition Universelle 1878*, 1881 (2 vols) *L'Exposition Universelle de 1878 Illustrée* 1879

1889 – PARIS   Exposition Universelle
The Official Report: *Rapport Général – Exposition Universelle 1889* (10 vols) 1890–92 (contains an excellent article on previous exhibitions in volume 1)
L'Exposition de Paris (1889) Publiée avec la Collaboration d'Ecrivains Spéciaux (4 vols – usually bound in 2 vols) 1889
Harriss, J. *The Tallest Tower – Eiffel and the Belle Epoque*, Houghton Mifflin Company, Boston, USA 1975

1893 – CHICAGO   World's Columbian Exposition
The Official Report: *Chicago 1893 – World's Columbian Exposition, Memorial Volume* 1893
The World's Fair in Watercolours by C. Graham, Sessler & Dungan 1893.
Burg, D. F. *Chicago's White City of 1893*, University Press of Kentucky 1976

1900 – PARIS   Exposition Universelle
The Official Report: *Rapport Général administratif et technique par Alfred Picard* (8 vols) 1902
Catalogue général officiel (20 vols) 1900
Paris 1900 – Exposition Universelle, Héliotypies de E. Le Deley 1900
L'Exposition de Paris (1900) Publiée avec la Collaboration d'Ecrivains Speciaux et des Meilleurs Artistes (6 vols – usually bound in 3 vols)
Mandell, R. D. *Paris 1900 – The Great World's Fair*, University of Toronto Press, Canada 1967 (contains an excellent bibliography)
Julian, P. *The Triumph of Art Nouveau – Paris Exhibition 1900* (English Edition – Phaidon Press, London 1974)

1904 – ST LOUIS   Louisiana Purchase Exposition
The Official Record: *The Universal Exposition of 1904* by David R. Francis (2 vols) 1913

Text references and acknowledgements

1915 – SAN FRANCISCO   Panama-Pacific Exposition
The Official Record: *The Story of the Exposition* . . . (5 vols) G. P. Putnam's
   Sons; New York & London 1921
The Exposition in Colors, Official Publication 1915
San Francisco's Wildflower – The Palace of Fine Arts, by E. E. Burden
   Phoenix Publishing. San Francisco 1967

1937 – PARIS   Exposition Internationale des Arts et Techniques dans la
Vie Moderne
The Official Record: *Livre d'Or Officiel de l'Exposition Internationale des
   Arts et techniques,* 1937
The Official Report: *Exposition Internationale des Arts et Techniques, Paris
   1937 – Rapport Générale* (10 vols) 1938

1939–40 – NEW YORK   New York World's Fair
The Official Report: *New York World's Fair, United States, 1939* . . .
Report to Congress of the United States, Washington 1941 (and
   supplement)

1958 – BRUSSELS   Exposition Universelle et Internationale de Bruxelles
The Official Record: *Le Memorial Officiel de L'Exposition Universelle et
   Internationale de Bruxelles* (8 vols) 1958

1967 – MONTREAL   Universal and International Exhibition
The Official Report: *The General Report on the 1967 World Exhibition* (5
   vols plus appendixes) Ottawa
The Official Record: *L'Album-Mémorial de L'Exposition Universelle et
   Internationale de Première Catégorie tenue à Montreal* ... Thomas
   Nelson: Toronto & Montreal 1968

1970 – OSAKA   Japan World Exposition
The Official Report: *Japan World Exposition, Osaka, 1970 – Official Report*
   (3 vols and 4 appendixes)
Official Photo Album – Japan World Exposition, Osaka, 1970 1971

The following books cover the whole subject.
Colmont, Achille de, *Histoire des Expositions des Produits de l'Industrie
   Française,* Paris: Guillaumin 1855
Cornell, Elias, *De Stora Utställingarna: Arkitekturexperiment och
   Kulturhistoria,* Stockholm: Natur och kultur 1952.
Isay, Raymond, *Panorama des Expositions Universelles,* Paris: Gallimard
   1937
Jaffé, Franz, *Handbuch der Architektur; Gebäude für Sammlungen und
   Ausstellungen,* Stuttgart 1906
Luckhurst, Kenneth W. *The Story of Exhibitions* London: Studio
   Publications 1951
Poirier, René, *Des Foires, des Peoples, des Expositions* Paris: Plon 1958
   Finally, there are many references to international exhibitions in
contemporary magazines and newspapers. Periodicals such as the
Illustrated London News (U.K.), *Harpers Bazaar* (U.S.A.), *The Art Journal*
(U.K.), *L'Illustration* (France), *Architectural Review* (U.K.), *L'Architecture
d'Aujourd'hui* (France) and many others are rich in both information and
illustrations.

The Author would like to thank all those who provided him with sources
for much of the contemporary comment on the Exhibitions and
particularly Lady Margaret Elton, C. H. Gibbs-Smith, Esq., Dr Stephen
Hadfield, Professor Dana S. Scott, Thomas Cook and Co. Ltd, EMI Music
Publishing Co. Ltd.

CHAPTER ONE

1 *My Circus Life* Lloyd, James. London, 1925
2 Official publicity brochure Expo '74, Spokane, USA, 1973
3 *Australian World Exposition Project Sponsors Report and Feasibility
   Study* Melbourne, Australia, 1966

CHAPTER TWO

1 *Fifty Years of Public Work* Cole, Sir Henry. London, 1884 (2 vols)
2 *Punch* magazine. London, 1850
3 The letters of His Royal Highness Prince Albert, The Royal Archives,
   Windsor Castle Library (by gracious permission of Her Majesty the
   Queen)
4 *May Day Ode* Thackeray, William Makepeace. 1851
5 Queen Victoria's Personal Diary, 1 May 1851, The Royal Archives,
   Windsor Castle Library (by gracious permission of Her Majesty the
   Queen)
6 Thackeray *op. cit.*
7 Official Jury Reports 1851
8 *ibid.*
9 *Nottingham Mercury and Midland Advertiser* 14 May 1851, page 2
   column 4

CHAPTER THREE

1 *Country Life* 15 March 1973 'Ireland's Great Exhibition'. Jones, Mark
   Bence
2 *The Exposition Expositer and Advertiser* ed. Sproule, J. Dublin. 1853 (24
   issues)
3 *The Masterpieces of the Centennial Exposition* Wilson, Joseph.
   Philadelphia, 1876 (3 vols)
4 *The Song of the Exposition* Whitman, Walt. 1853
5 Diary of George Templeton Strong of New York (*Crystal Palace/42
   Street/1853–54*): City University Graduate Centre, New York, 1974
6 Wilson, *op. cit.*
7 Wilson, *op. cit.*
8 *Art in Paris 1845–1862,* Baudelaire, Charles (reprint – Phaidon Press,
   London 1965)
9 *Art Journal,* Exhibition Catalogue 1855
10 *The Illustrated Catalogue of the International Exhibition* London, 1862
   (4 vols)

CHAPTER FOUR

1 *Rapport sur l'Exposition Universelle de 1855* Paris, 1857
2 *The Masterpieces of the Centennial Exposition* Wilson, Joseph. Philadelphia, 1876 (3 vols)
3 *ibid.*
4 Royal Society of Arts Journal, Vol XV (5 April 1867)
5 *Journal de E. de Goncourt* Paris, 1867
6 *The Illustrated History of the Centennial Exhibition* . . . McCabe, James D. Philadelphia, 1876

CHAPTER FIVE

1 *Art Journal* Exhibition Catalogue, 1878
2 *Paris Herself Again* Sala, George Augustus. London, 1880 (2 vols)
3 The private diaries of Mr George Hadfield of Ross-on-Wye
4 Sala, George Augustus *op. cit.*
5 Sala, George Augustus *op. cit.*
6 *Victoria and its Metropolis* Melbourne (volume 1)
7 *ibid.*
8 *ibid.*

CHAPTER SIX

1 The private diaries of Mr George Hadfield of Ross-on-Wye
2 *ibid.*
3 *ibid.*
4 *Official Exposition Guide Book* Chicago, 1893
5 *ibid.*
6 *Shepp's World's Fair Photographic* Chicago, 1893
7 *ibid.*
8 *Richards and Elliott* Howe, Julia Ward
9 Text on the exhibition fascia of the *'49 Mining Camp* concession San Francisco, 1894

CHAPTER SEVEN

1 *Journal d'un Nègre à l'Exposition* Bergeret, Gaston. Paris 1901
2 *The Times* 14 May 1901
3 Bergeret, Gaston *op. cit.*
4 Hachette's '1900 Almanach'
5 *Passenger Conveyors* Tough, John and O'Flaherty, Coleman. London, 1971

CHAPTER EIGHT

1 *Meet Me in St Louis, Louis* popular song, words by Stirling, A., music by Mills, Kerry
2 *The Universal Exposition of 1904* Francis, D. R. St Louis, 1913
3 Contemporary postcard from the author's collection
4 *Palaces and Courts of the Exposition* . . . James, Juliet. San Francisco, 1915
5 *ibid.*
6 *ibid.*
7 *ibid.*

CHAPTER NINE

1 The Official Guidebook to the British Empire Exhibition London, 1924
2 *ibid.*
3 *ibid.*
4 *ibid.*
5 *Exhibitions and the Art of Display* Weaver, Sir Lawrence. London, 1925
6 Official guidebook to Century of Progress Exposition, Chicago, 1933
7 *The Paris Exposition of 1937* International Chamber of Commerce minute. Washington DC, 1937
8 *ibid.*
9 *ibid.*
10 *The International Exhibition of Arts and Crafts – Paris 1937* Publicity Department minute, Metropolitan-Vickers Electrical Co. Ltd. Manchester, 1937
11 *ibid.*

CHAPTER TEN

1 *Architectural Review* 15 June 1939
2 *ibid.*
3 Official Guide Book New York World's Fair 1939–40

CHAPTER ELEVEN

1 *Electronic Poem* Le Corbusier (*International Lighting Review* No. 3/4 1958)
2 *Century 21 – The Story of the Seattle World's Fair 1962* Morgan, M. Seattle, 1963
3 *National Geographic Magazine* Washington DC 1962
4 Morgan, M. *op. cit.*

CHAPTER TWELVE

1 Inscription on the plaque at the base of the 'Unisphere', Flushing Meadow Park, New York City
2 *Le Monde Illustré* Montreal 4 May 1895
3 *Film as Environment* . . . Chew, William (*Architectural Association Review*, vol. 6 No. 3/4, London 1974)
4 Buckminster Fuller describing his design
5 Chew, William *op. cit.*

191